# LOOK BACK IN JOY

Malcolm Boyd

Malcolm Boyd
Photo © 1980 Roger Ressmeyer

# LOOK BACK IN JOY

## CELEBRATION OF GAY LOVERS

Malcolm Boyd

Gay Sunshine Press
San Francisco

First edition 1981
Copyright © 1981 by Malcolm Boyd
Photos © 1980 Roger Ressmeyer
Interview © 1980 by Edward Curtin, Jr.
"The Bishop" is reprinted with permission from *The Advocate*. Copyright ©
1980 Liberation Publications Inc.

Cover design by Frank Holbrook

Library of Congress Cataloging in Publication Data:

Boyd, Malcolm, 1923–
   Look back in joy.

   1. Boyd, Malcolm, 1923–.  2. Homosexuals,
Male—United States—Biography.  3. Homosexuality—
United States. I. Title.
HQ75.8.B68A34    306.7'6'0924  [B]   81-2177
ISBN 0-917342-85-2          AACR2
ISBN 0-917342-77-1 (pbk.)

Gay Sunshine Press
P.O. Box 40397
San Francisco, CA 94140
Write for free catalogue of titles available.

# TABLE OF CONTENTS

Love me! Love me! I called—in sounds of hurt and fury—to strangers. I discovered then the curiosity of love. Love is not taken or given. I found it can be shared.

To
JOHN A. DUE

I traveled around a great deal. The cities swept about me like dead leaves, leaves that were brightly colored but torn away from the branches.

I would have stopped, but I was pursued by something.

Tom, in *The Glass Menagerie*
by Tennessee Williams

Past midnight. Never knew—

Samuel Beckett, *Krapp's Last Tape*

Then he said, "Let me go, for the day is breaking." But Jacob said, "I will not let you go, unless you bless me."

Genesis, 32:26

# SPRING

# A CERTAIN FORMALITY

In the city on a visit, I sat in an arcade of one of the great hotels. I sipped coffee, partially read a newspaper, partially eyed the men who passed by.

Suddenly, there he was. Slim, understated in an easy elegance, smiling diffidently as always. He shook my hand, greeting me publicly with a certain formality. Yet I had known every form of erotic intimacy with him.

We chatted. I remembered our unabashedly open times together. Once on a trip to the mountains we spent hour after hour making love. He was direct and forceful, yet gentle and slower than poured thick honey, an alien to unseemly haste.

Another time we stayed a week in a fleabag hotel in a rundown, forgotten section of the city where we were lost to the world outside us. The clock did not rule us; only our senses did. We laughed insanely on city streets, walked in the pouring rain, went to a movie in the morning, ate breakfast for dinner and a hamburger at dawn. We never wanted to leave each other.

Now, he said, he was on his way to an appointment. I looked at him as if for the first time, caught the easy laughter in his eyes, the unabashed invitation that his body kindly sent to mine. He asked me to lunch the next day.

# SIGNALS

He meticulously wore shades whenever he was out in public in the daytime. He tried to convey an offhand, cool impression, but the deep torment in his life never let him carry it off well.

Yet his tinted dark glasses curiously granted him identity by seeming to obscure it. They also met his need to feel separated from the mainstream of life even as it flowed all around him.

At first, I misunderstood the signals he sent me. I assumed that they were inviting. Only when I grasped the underlying anguish and brittle vulnerability of his life, did I realize the meaning of the warnings he had quietly given me to stay away.

At surface social levels he functioned very properly. His smile was quick, conversation ready and animated enough, dress an inconspicuous uniform: he wore jeans that were not tight.

The one time he restrainedly kissed and held me, as we stood in the living room of his apartment, I sensed the agony of his control, the burden of his lack of spontaneity. He did not possess the capacity to be hurt again.

We became, and remained, friends. I never brought him close to the fire, never singed his reserve.

# THE PROFESSOR

He was a professor, I a student, at a distinguished theological seminary.

For months I had felt the insistent pressure of his eyes upon me, a word of special greeting in classroom and hallway, a smile that mixed a suggestion of lust with professorial kindness.

Unexpectedly, we ran into each other in the seminary post office where we picked up our mail. Could I come by his apartment the next Sunday at five for a drink, he asked.

From that moment until the date itself, I entertained the wildest fantasies about what might happen on Sunday afternoon. I tossed in bed, unable to get to sleep. His mouth and mustache were sensuous, his eyes liquid, his body a muscular challenge. So much was innuendo and unspoken in our casual meetings, that suggestion took over in my consciousness.

I was not disappointed on the next Sunday. He was masterful in his first kiss inside the door, disrobing me, leading me to his bed. There, we were equals. But ever afterward, outside of bed, he had always to play the professor.

# FIRST KISS

What if I hadn't bestowed it? Would we have ever seen each other again?

We had met the night before at a public dinner where I was (as seemed almost inevitable in those days of urgent celebrity) the guest speaker. I quietly told him that the next day would be my birthday. I hoped he would want to share it with me.

When he showed up at my apartment I was more delighted than surprised. I had made no birthday plans and was alone. We sparred conversationally for a while. I mixed drinks. I knew that he liked me as much as I liked him. How would it be possible to break the ice and cut below the banalities of our conventional discussion?

I studied his face, his eyes, mouth, lips, skin, eyebrows, hair. I found his energy, humor and personality irresistible. Yet I still held back. What if he wasn't gay? What if his laughing eyes quickly turned to anger, and he struck me and walked out?

So, we talked on and on. About nothing. Yet the form of our conversation took on a certain sophistication. Clearly, a game was being played. His eyes expressed a deep longing.

I kissed him.

We stayed together for a long, long time, and our love never died.

We were lovers for years. Even after we separated for professional and geographical reasons, our love never died.

# SUNSHINE

We were in high school.

I was the most insecure youth on earth. He was the quarterback of the school football team, student body president, and a young god.

He was also—incongruously, and for a while—my best friend. I found qualities in him that people who saw only his persona never knew. He was insecure, vulnerable and honest. These factors would later reshape his life, bringing him personal happiness that refused to make its peace with social mores of success.

I was mad about him, but never said so. We spent hours together—talking endlessly, rowing on a lake, walking. I basked in his company and masculine beauty. A sensuousness hung low over our friendship. His movements were slow, easy, natural; his smile full of honey and sunshine. I ached with desire for him, yet never broke the macho bond by touching his body with passion or speaking to him about my feelings.

The years passed. I saw him once. He was with his wife and children, en route to a far corner of the world where he would work. He was stripped to the waist, barefoot, uninhibited, laughing.

I still longed for him.

# SANCTUARY

Religious objects filled the room. There were icons, crosses, paintings of Jesus and the saints. The smell of burning incense added to the sanctuary-like atmosphere.

This was his bedroom. He was a recent convert to Anglo-Catholicism from fundamentalistic Protestantism.

Also, he was gay, exuberant, and every inch of his body seemed packed with electric energy. He reminded me of what I had read about quite mad ancient Christian zealots who roamed the desert and were inflamed by life.

His lambent eyes flickered with an uneasy brilliance. They seemed to be mirrors of a soul that was wild.

A red sanctuary lamp burned brightly in his room as we made love. He planned to study for the priesthood. I wondered why he didn't wear a chasuble as he lay on the bed, or play Gregorian Chant as a musical background for our scene.

# TEASING

It got lonely, and mostly very boring, when I lived in a student dormitory in graduate school.

He was a successful public relations man in a downtown firm. We met by chance, and our eyes communicated an implicit shorthand. Soon, he invited me to his luxurious apartment.

Afterward, he called from time to time. Always I caught a subway and went to his place near the Village where I spent the night, returning to my student world the next morning.

He was outgoing and generous. Our sex had a lot of play in it. We bathed together in a huge tub, soaping and rubbing each other, laughing and teasing. We frolicked in his enormous four-poster bed, never taking ourselves too seriously.

Some years later, I ran into him quite by accident at a party. Both of us had changed. I was self-assured where I had been reliant upon others, poised instead of shy. On the other hand, he had grown soft and flabby, and lacked his former sharp focus.

He wanted me to spend the night with him. I couldn't. He broke down and cried. I felt a bit guilty, then grew angry about the situation. Finally, I simply felt pity for him. But since then I have always wished that I could have made such splendid love to him as to have brought back his former élan, spring, control, beauty, firmness, that good feeling about himself.

# THE LABORING MEN

A cousin of mine, a U.S. businessman who was as straight as American Gothic, took me with him on a short auto trip into Italy.

I tried to disguise my sharp looks in the direction of lusty Italian men, finally endeavoring not to look at all after my cousin expressed implicit disapproval. But this made me tense and edgy. My cousin and I, sharing a hotel room at nights and spending hours alone in his car during the days, began to fall into long, awkward periods of silence.

He was keenly aware of something different in me that he did not like. I was frustrated and miserable. We found little to talk or laugh about.

Near the end of our journey, as we drove in his open convertible along a highway near Milan, we were behind an open truck occupied by five laboring men. They were stripped to the waist, revealing bare, bronzed shoulders and lean bodies. My intent gaze caught the eye of one man. His sensuousness responded with alacrity to mine. He winked at me, smiled broadly, and happily caressed one of his bare nipples. I smiled back and started to make gestures of friendship.

My cousin became furious. He gunned the car's motor, took a dangerous swerve around the truck on the narrow road, and raced toward our destination. Not another word was said between us on the journey.

# THE LETTER

When I read the letter, I was touched and also aroused.

A stranger, yet someone whom I knew by his fame, he wrote to tell me that he'd had an erotic dream about me—about us together.

Knowing that I would shortly visit the city where he lived, I wrote to let him know.

The morning arrived when he knocked on the door of my hotel room. After I greeted him, we sat and talked. Yet the intimacy and charged feeling contained in his letter were woefully absent from our exchange.

I walked across the space that separated us, touched his body and caressed his face. Within a few moments we held each other, naked, on the bed.

He was a prince among men, possessing inner as well as outer beauty. His full beard made him resemble an Old Testament prophet. We were able to enjoy long silences, infinite pauses, the absence of pretense and conscious performance.

I felt that I had known him all my life in the profound biblical sense of sharing his soul as well as his body.

# START AND FINISH

Beginnings in a relationship can be awkward, time-consuming, interesting, and lead toward involvement.

Endings tend to be wise, functional and sad.

However, the beginning of our relationship was easy and quick, and we were plunged without warning into an involvement that made us lovers for two years.

Our break-up was awful, a classic act of torment and turmoil.

The end was yet to come. On a visit to Honolulu, where he had moved, I acted on the spur of the moment and telephoned him. To my surprise, the call was an extremely pleasant one. Apparently our angst was behind us. He asked me to dinner.

When I saw him, I was instantly aware that I felt nothing but love. I remembered only the good parts of our life together.

The evening in Honolulu, probably the last time I would ever see him, was not sad at all. Nor was it particularly wise or functional. We partied entirely too much, throwing caution to the winds. We laughed and were overjoyed. The hell with roles; we were simply ourselves.

# GREAT EXPECTATIONS

The ballroom was packed with people attending a banquet. I saw him across the room. He sat at the head table and, as chairperson of the event, introduced guest dignitaries and speakers. I wanted to know him. To my delight, I ran into him quite by chance on a street the next week. We stopped, acted surprised, and chatted easily.

It seemed providential that I saw him soon again at a small, informal party. After we talked for a while, I asked him to have dinner with me. Yes, he'd like that very much. We picked a date. When it had to be changed, I realize in retrospect that it was a bad omen, but at the time I paid no attention.

At the designated hour he arrived at my place. We drank chilled white wine and went out to dinner.

However, something was wrong. We sat at the table like two heads of day-old lettuce. What had happened to the excitement I had felt? It was gone; he was absolutely dull; he must have thought that I was, too.

Long silences punctuated dinner. There was nothing to talk about. Finally, there was nothing even to think of. We yawned over coffee.

Coming home, we said goodbye, exchanged a limp kiss, said we must see each other again soon.

# THE VALKYRIE

The air changed that night from cold to warm. Spring arrived in its predictably spontaneous fashion. I knew, of course, that it couldn't last. Always it comes and goes so quickly. But I savored its seductiveness, its embrace and spicy smells.

Just then I met an athletic, ardent Navy chaplain. Every night after we made love, he held me in his arms, refusing to stop and go to sleep.

One day we went to the shore of a lake. The sun was hot, a breeze blowing, as we stripped naked and our bodies united on the sand. I half expected a Wagnerian horn to sound an alarm, and dozens of Valkyrie to rush upon us from a nearby hill, but only the sound of the waves intruded on our erotic consciousness.

Years later, after an eon of silence, he sent me a Christmas card.

# MACHO

In college I belonged to the most macho fraternity on the campus. It had most of the members of the football team, basketball team, baseball team, swimming team, golf team—virtually everything but the tennis team.

I was different.

He was different, too, and a member of the same fraternity. Years later, I was told that he was gay. This, after he had committed suicide when arrested on a homosexual charge while in military service.

I remember that he was blond, husky with broad shoulders, and laughed a lot. I cannot recall ever seeing him depressed or caught in evident anxiety. The face he showed that world was a happy one.

As fraternity brothers in college, neither of us understood our sexual orientation. It was there, but something to be overlooked, brushed aside, secretly worried about (at least, on my part), never talked about. So, we did not discuss or share it.

However, the sole enjoyment I had was with him. We slipped away from everyone else and shared our laughter about them. We held a common view of the absurdity of campus life, its myths and rituals.

I wish that we had been liberated enough to know each other. If we had, it might have been a strong enough factor to keep him from committing suicide later. I shall always mourn his death and wish he had been able to live in an accepting society.

# PURE REASON

I asked myself: Is my life careening madly down a speeding track? Have I lost all control?

Just then, when I was full of anxious emotion and unchanneled passion, I met a man of pure reason and apparently imperturbably inner peace. He was two dozen boy scouts, sans uniforms, in one six-foot Scandinavian body, with blond hair and perfect intelligence.

When I tried to introduce him to feeling, he veered straight back to clear linear lines of rational thought. It became apparent to me that maintaining rigid control over his life was as natural for him as breathing. If he ever really let go, he might drop over a wall like Humpty Dumpty, and smash.

He analyzed everything—words that described feelings, people's reactions, possible alternatives to life courses. A successful young banker, he thought that he wanted marvelous far-flung adventures—but knew deep inside his mind that he did not.

I left this beautiful creature inside a cozily warm apartment working on a complicated crossword puzzle, as I went walking in the wind-lashed spring rain.

# THE OPERA

Always we made love before we went to the opera.

Our night on the subscription series was Wednesdays. So, on the late afternoons we got inside the covers and relished each other. After that, a light supper with a glass of wine. Then, off to the opera.

*Norma. La Boheme. Tosca. Fidelio. Der Rosenkavalier. Turandot. Lohengrin. Don Carlo. La Gioconda.* At intermissions the men attending the opera, dressed in everything from tuxedos to jeans, took close measure of one another climbing the marble stairs or conversing under the great chandelier. Always we waited for the coming of the last intermission to drink a glass of champagne.

The sadness of *La Boheme* brought tears to my eyes. So did the trio in the final act of *Der Rosenkavalier.* I suppose it is fortunate that *Tristan und Isolde* was not on our series, with its tragic if transcendent Liebestod.

To spill over with emotion is something that I have always done in the presence of beauty that touches me in an opera, at the theatre or a museum. I savor the sense that it is my likeness to Zorba.

Yet I could not dance to express my grief when we parted.

# MOVING DAY

Bare walls, empty rooms, rugs up, pictures down. On this moving day, I wondered if my breath or footsteps had left any kind of mark to indicate my passing life in those rooms.

That evening, friends asked me to dine with them. It was a relief to get away from unpacked crates of books and stacks of plates wrapped in newspaper on a sink.

I arrived early at their home. He met me at the door and explained that his lover would arrive late from the office. After he poured us drinks, and we sat side by side on a couch, he reached out with his hand and touched my bare arm. His fingers caressed my hairs and flesh.

We were plunged into a maelstrom of sensation and ecstasy in that formal room with its drapes, oil paintings and collection of jade.

Later, over dinner, the three of us discussed presidential politics.

# THE RAINS CAME

He had shining, explosive, dark eyes. His body was lithe, his smile warm and open. We met in a Greenwich Village bar.

Explaining that his father and mother were away, and the house he shared with them was empty, he invited me to his home in a distant suburb. We boarded a train and reached our destination after what seemed an interminable length of time. We were maddeningly ready to tear off our clothes and make love.

He unlocked the front door and opened it. As we walked inside the house, excited voices rang out. His parents' plans had obviously changed, and they were at home. He and his family were clearly involved in a crisis of dire proportions. He begged me to leave immediately, for my presence was proof that he was gay.

Out on the street, I realized it had begun to rain hard. I did not have any idea where I was. For hours I walked block after block, each containing similar locked, dark houses. No phone booth was in sight. I was drenched.

I walked all night. Half-drowned, chilled, and shaken by laughter at the lunacy of my predicament, I managed to hitchhike a ride into Manhattan in a truck.

What had I learned? Never trust a stranger? Yet I knew that would mean I could not trust anyone.

# SUMMER

# THE MAN ON THE ROAD

Driving along the Mediterranean from Cannes to Monaco, I noticed the flowers in bloom along the road. The sun shone on the blue sea below.

He walked on the side of the road ahead. When he turned to cross the road, I slowed the car.

It was then I saw him, my quintessential ideal of male beauty. He seemed perfectly formed without self-conscious excess or arrogance. His movements were graceful and natural.

Our eyes met for an instant.

I seemed to gaze into the depths of an ocean, a rose, softly falling snow, an idyllic forest. I loved him.

He returned my look with simplicity, openness and acceptance. He focussed intently on me, shutting out the world, expressing love and desire.

I have already driven past him on the road., helplessly as if I were drowning. Should I have braked the car, run back and taken him in my arms under the noon sun?

I drove back to the same place on the road the next day, and the next, and the next, but did not find him again.

# SLEEP

The scene was like a gigantic medieval fair. Africans, Asians, Europeans, Americans, Latins and Australians mixed. The crowds were too large, meetings and lines too long, and everyone grew a bit tired.

I was in Europe to attend an international conference of Christian students. One morning I was in a densely packed cathedral for a religious service.

Amid pomp and pomposity, singing by massed choirs and tedious speeches, I became keenly interested in the man seated next to me. A black American, he spoke softly to me about making love as soon as we were back in our student dormitory. To the accompaniment of liturgical words and music, we touched.

He had a great head of black hair, a splendid mustache, a Pharaoh's profile and a friendly smile. Our growing sense of urgency to be alone together was met by ever more speeches, further introductions of dignitaries, longer musical offerings. The summer's heat inside the cathedral was stifling. I noticed finally that he began to nod his head.

When the service ended, we walked to my small room in the dormitory, got out of our clothes and lay on the bed. However, soon his head nodded again. As his snores broke like thunder through the room's silence, he was lost to sleep and me.

# THE ROOMMATE

I arrived in New York City late in the afternoon and went directly to the Harvard Club where I was to stay as a guest for a few days.

But, to be alone on my first night in New York was intolerable. What could I do?

I remembered a face, a handsome one with a quizzical, searching look. I paired it with an apartment in Sutton Place. I had stopped there briefly once with a friend with whom I had an affair. The remembered face, it belonged to our host that evening long ago. Could I find him again?

Like a Marco Polo, I tracked my way carefully to the east side—and, yes, the building. I found a name that looked familiar on the lobby mailbox, then took the elevator up to the floor and rang the bell. When the door opened, the romantic face greeted me with a smile.

I spent my first night in New York with the man behind the face. He was charming, a delight to be with. However, when I met his roommate, my heart danced.

# COMPLINE

I shared a house one night with a young priest who had asked me to stay. I knew that he was gay and assumed because of the invitation that he was open to me as a lover.

However, when I kissed him, I heard a story of his still unresolved sexuality. The priest had been hurt badly in a brief relationship with another man. He was extremely vulnerable right now, sensitive to the point of feeling acute pain in reaching out to another person. Not yet ready to have sexual relations with anyone, he believed that he was in the process of being healed.

Shortly he made up a bed for me in a room adjoining his own. When I looked in to tell him goodnight, the priest lay in his bed reading psalms for Compline. Our gayness was shared in an open, loving, supportive way without sexual expression.

Later, he told me that he found a lover, and was able to share an open and healthy relationship with him.

# GREEN BRITCHES, WHITE PLUMES

Sea gulls circled overhead. The ocean at Malibu was a resplendent army wearing green britches and white plumes. The soldiers moved in a ritualized, brisk choreography as the waves broke snappily on the shore.

The sounds of the sea rushed through my ears.

We were so happy, having banished every care in the world. He was into middle age, Bogartian and wise. He had worked as a producer in Hollywood for years, was eternally tanned, a celebrity without making a point of it, a raconteur, gourmet, sophisticate, and international traveler.

Curiously, it was his innate shyness that made him attractive to me. His eyes belonged to an El Greco painting, and he was immensely tender. I realized soon that he no longer gave away all of himself. However, relaxed and happy, he almost did with me.

# BORROWED TIME

Lights from anchored ships in the harbor sent silvery traces over the tide toward us as we lay on a deserted San Francisco wharf.

He held me in his arms, and I was grateful once again to realize that our delight needed no stimulus. Yet both of us recognized that we were on borrowed time. This lent a bittersweet note to our happiness.

He was married. We had met in a bar when his wife was out of town, and I had gone home to their small apartment. Our lovemaking was ecstasy. We breathed into each other's nostrils, smelling our essence. We wrestled and tasted, drank each other and laughed.

We met many times afterward. His body resembled that of a chiseled marble Greek warrior. His manner was shy, his laughter intimate and easy.

We used to walk across the Golden Gate Bridge, looking down at the white caps far below. Finally, during our last walk together there, we said goodbye.

# HUSTLER

He was a hustler, and I didn't know it. When I found out, I didn't care. I liked him. But, I lost an expensive watch.

I had come to the Riviera and was lonely. The sea. The moon. The crowds of people. I wanted to be with someone. I can't remember how I met him. I assumed that he was attracted to me. He stayed with me for two days. (It's amazing he didn't take my car, my clothes, my billfold, my travelers cheques. He must have liked me, too).

We did a lot of things. Swam. Walked along the beach. Ate bouillabaisse. Drank wine. Talked quite a lot. I told him all about myself. He told me everything about himself except his present occupation.

The third day, in the morning, I dropped him off someplace he'd asked to go on an errand. (That morning in bed he had asked me if he could wear my watch. I said yes, and gave it to him). When he didn't come out of the building after a few minutes, I honked the horn. I went to find him. But I never did. I never saw him again.

I'm glad he had the watch, as a memento of me. I genuinely liked him. His unspoiled youth was poignant, especially when I looked into his eyes as we made love.

# SOUND OF TIRES ON WET PAVEMENT

Awakening in the hotel room, I heard the hiss of tires moving over wet pavement on the street outside. The cacophony of distant motors, punctuated by an occasional horn, insinuated itself in my consciousness.

I was in Madrid, and lay in bed with a medical student. A young Puerto Rican, he was the epitome of grace. We were inseparable during my visit. One afternoon, when he couldn't be with me, he sent his best friend, a Spaniard, to keep me company and make love. It was very idealistic and beautiful.

But this morning, as the medical student lay sleeping contentedly in my arms, and I listened to the sound of tires on the wet pavement outside, I was reminded sharply of the transitory quality of our lives.

I knew that I would depart tomorrow and never see him again.

# TRIO

That afternoon it occurred to me with stunning clarity that the journey into self is like the Mongolian desert: remote, arid, very, very hard, and quite perplexing. I chose to take the way out of myself.

Two lovers had asked me to stay with them. One, twenty-seven, worked as a telephone line repairman. The other, thirty-three, divorced after years of marriage and raising a family, was an artist.

The three of us seemed prepared for our relationship by destiny. There was no tinge of jealousy or hurt feeling, but only equal sharing and pleasure.

I was the only man who had ever slept between their bodies in bed at night. Awakening occasionally to spontaneous movements of provocation and delight, we worked out sleeping positions that complemented three bodies instead of two.

A trio, I found, can be infinitely richer in tone and rhythm than a duet.

# AN OLD FRIEND

The intensity of seeing him again made me drive the car with dangerous abandon.

Our time together would be no more than an hour. I drove across France from Paris, accompanied by two people who did not know of my feeling for him, or what emotions were aroused in me by making the trip.

His life was settled now. He was well-known. Our brief reunion would have to appear utterly casual and low-key, almost as if it were something trivial and entirely by chance.

So, as I drove the car, I talked of every possible subject except the one that mattered to me. My two companions must have wondered about the frenzy of my driving, yet my seemingly relaxed laughter no doubt kept them from worrying about it.

When we reached our destination, the three of us had lunch, shopped, went through the ritual of sightseeing. Then, I mentioned that I wanted to look up an old friend just to say hello, if he happened to be in. Could we meet in an hour? They went off to see a church or a castle, I to see him.

We held each other. I hoped that my eyes would be clear after shedding tears when I rejoined my companions.

I searched his life, he mine. Everything to do, say, feel, experience in an hour. Sixty minutes.

Then, somehow I said goodbye and walked away.

# SHY AND BOLD

I was angry, fatigued, lonely and very frustrated. It was a marvelous combination of feelings to precede a romance.

Alone without my lover, I was attending a conference in the midwest in the dead of summer. I felt the additional pressure of being the principal speaker there.

I longed for companionship. When I saw him, I sincerely hoped that I had found it. We were introduced. He was pleasant but noncommital. I moved in on my quarry, as if I were the Great Hunter.

He had a mixture of vulnerable shyness and direct boldness that I found inviting. I asked him to go dancing that night. We found a gay disco with exploding sound and maddening energy. We danced like war horses.

Our night together in his room was so beautiful that I lost my anger, fatigue, loneliness and frustration. The young priest truly gave me peace.

# THE KEY

We drove up the Oregon coast into Washington, then headed for Seattle.

We stayed at the "Y."

I had known him for years, yet he was a stranger to me. He was a tortured enigma of a man, a combination of loner with a short fuse of anger and sophisticated extrovert who generated the laughs in a crowd.

He was rugged, physically handsome and in control: he did the driving, made most of the decisions about our trip, and I settled back and enjoyed not having to think.

We stayed in Seattle for several days. During the days we saw the sights, and he introduced me to a couple of friends of his who were women. I sensed the sadness they felt about him, the inability of such a sexually arousing man to become aroused by them. It was clear that they saw him as a Gary Cooper or a Steve McQueen, and that he had no idea what they felt about him.

At night, we drank. Heavily. We moved from bar to bar. Then we returned to the "Y" and fell on our narrow cots. I couldn't find the key to unlock the truth buried in him.

Why couldn't we make love instead of drink? Because he was afraid, sorely afraid, and I knew that if I touched the live wire an explosion could blow us up.

# EARLY MORNING

The party had been a wonder, a natural mix of blacks and whites, women and men, gays and straights, the intolerably rich and the intolerably poor.

It was held in an old boarding house in the inner-city of Detroit. The neighborhood was known to be dangerous. The house was honeycombed with people who rented rooms there. Our host was someone whom we all knew in a civil rights organization in the early sixties.

A strong awareness of the house's decadence contributed more to the high spirit of the party than its flowing liquor. We sat on ragged velvet cushions on the floor of a small room that hemmed us in tightly. A crystal chandelier that had seen better days cast a faded light on the scene.

When everyone else had departed, I stayed and slept there.

Early morning light coming through the window awakened me. The sun was already very, very hot. I heard a bird sing in a tree outside. Then he opened the door and came to me.

# GLAMOR

Jumping out of bed on our first morning in Venice, I looked outside the window. Waves washed the stone steps of a nearby palace, a romantic edifice whose colors of rose, pink and faded orange filled my eyes. It was a scene of enchantment, casting a magic spell.

Barges filled with men and goods moved along the water of the canal. Sounds on the canal were loud.

We had long wished to make this visit to Venice. Now, he lay sleeping, oblivious of the coming of the new day. Our dream of the trip held compelling charm for both of us, yet ever present realities impinged on our innocent joy.

God willing, our love would survive the rigors of being tourists together: back aches and head colds as well as glamorous dinners; enjoying moments of unforgettable inspiration, then returning to wash our clothes in the tiny basin of our closet-size bathroom; beholding the wonders of Western civilization while combating diarrhea.

# UNDER A FULL MOON

All that day the sun was an angry god, the ten commandments were harsh in the cloudless Spanish sky, the creed was a hot stone baking in the dusty ground.

Evening brought cool sanctuary. Yet I can't remember how we got onto his tile roof.

He was a dancer, I was visiting his home in Madrid, and somehow we were naked and making love on the tiles under a full moon. A bucket of iced champagne stood beside us.

He was dark and slim, imaginative and bold in the ways of loving. His practiced touch and kisses were those of the Arabian Nights. I kept seeing his laughing eyes close to mine in the moonlight that resembled a mysterious waterfall from the stars.

A few hours later, black coffee replaced the champagne, and we said goodbye. I was on my way to meet a date for a bullfight.

# ANGEL OF LIGHT

Walking on a desert at sunrise, I saw the rim of the sun come close to the horizon. The clouds in the sky changed from pearl to silver. When the sun exploded in the heavens, suddenly I felt enveloped by its hot flames.

I was wholeheartedly in love.

We held each other as if there had never been two young lovers in all the world before us. He was, in my eyes, far more beautiful than the most dazzling angel of light. His touch awakened my body, as if I had been sleeping for centuries and waited for him to come and save me.

On occasions we fought angrily, then reconciled with great and heightened tenderness. He was intensely and lustily human. We were inseparable for a while. I could not imagine my life continuing without him.

Yet soon our responsibilities would call us away from each other. He was a monk, I a priest. The church did not bless such a union. One wonders: did it prefer hiddenness, shame, guilt, and broken lives?

Writing about ourselves years later, I recollected: when you were gone, I felt lost within the whole world. I knew you were in it, too, but you weren't a part of me.

# NO MORE SADNESS

Cable cars. Nob Hill. Chinatown. North Beach. The Presidio. Land's End. I was back in San Francisco on a visit to address a conference.

Gradually, very gradually, I had begun the process of coming out as a gay man who was proud, not ashamed, of his sexuality.

I met a warm, sensuous man who invited me to Sunday brunch at a restaurant. After sipping a cocktail, we dined on buffet foods. Before coffee, the man told me that he had an early afternoon appointment. So, our time together was limited.

I suggested that we skip dessert and return to my room. Arriving there, we made brief but highly satisfying love. Soon our time had passed.

"I'm sorry," he said.

"Don't," I told him. "I feel only happiness. There has been too much sorrow. No more sadness. No more."

# AUTUMN

# A STUDY IN COLOR

I smelled the smoke that I saw rise in the air from burning leaves.

We had driven up to Vermont from New York for a few days before saying goodbye. He must return to college in California, I must leave for Europe.

His blackness burned in the night's dark and in my awareness. I believed that he made my whiteness appear pallid, washed-out, lacking definition. Yet our blackness and whiteness together created a pattern that both of us found intriguing.

Once during our trip we parked the car. We walked inside the woods alongside the road. When we held each other, and the realization that our time was so short stunned me anew, I began to sob.

Without warning, a hunter appeared. He was embarrassed to see two men in a tight embrace of love, and quickly vanished through the trees. Or, did he see us as a study in color?

# URBAN

5:30 p.m. There is free movement of people running.

People have been cooped-up all day inside office buildings. Now they rush, dance, flee, race for a date, a car or bus, home, a sandwich, a look into a store window. The mood is up, the tempo quick.

The feeling of expectancy is contagious. You have to run in order to avoid being trampled. The twenty-four hour period is back to origins, to scratch. An enormous momentum of life is building with the energy of the Yangtze River, and nothing will be able to stop it. The sheer power of masses of people in movement in every part of the city is staggering, overwhelming, electric and irresistible.

We felt it.

He was a Jewish intern at a Los Angeles hospital. We met quite by chance in a drugstore. There was no time!

We raced to his apartment. The sounds of a TV newscast in the next apartment punctuated the movements of our bodies and minds. An electric clock over the bed indicated the passing of each moment: 5:31, 5:32, 5:33; eternity closed in rapidly.

We behaved as conditioned urban creatures. Present Shock was our ambience.

# THE COUCH

He was after me. He wanted me, I knew.

A seminarian, closeted and guilt-ridden simply because of my feelings, I wasn't about to succumb to his advances—which I reasoned would surely make me feel even more guilty.

He was at every church function where I was given responsibilities. A devout layman, his presence was taken for granted by my superiors. However, he always managed to be in the men's room, and the parking lot late at night and an empty classroom, when I was there. He touched my body insinuatingly, laughed at me, tried to arouse me.

I was furious, but also horny and intrigued. What would it be *like?*

When I spent several months at a monastery, he also came there as a retreatant. His real purpose was to see me. He haunted me there, hunting me up and down monastery corridors, in chapels and gardens.

Deciding that I would wait for my lover to appear, I eluded him. I found a space behind an old couch in the monastery library. It was beneath a great window which afforded me the necessary light to read. So, I sat quietly behind the old couch for hour upon hour, devouring books.

He was dismayed by the mystery of my absence. At last, he left both the monastery and my life.

# ALONE

Two baleful but secretly loving eyes peered at me from a sturdy trunk. I visited a favorite tree of mine in search of refuge and peace. The tree understood me, and did not dismiss me with impatience or refuse to listen.

My relationship of two years had just been smashed as if it were a glass at a drunken party. I loved the man even though I realized that our love possessed organic problems that could never be solved. I would shortly be alone again.

How to preserve my sanity? How to survive the deep pain? I touched the tree as if it were my only friend. I stayed there a long while.

# SAMURAI

The meeting of East and West was, I found, exotic. He was Japanese-American. We seemed to be as happy as two peas in a pleasant pod.

In my romantic fantasy, I found him a marvelously affectionate member of the samurai.

Sex with him was a glorious adventure full of scarlet sunsets and starry skies. Violent in bed, he seized the fullness of time as well as me. I seized him, too, but we also engaged in hours of easy, spendthrift loving. Such ease. Such a languorous experience.

Time stopped.

# KING

I was utterly in love with him, would have done anything he wanted, including following him to the ends of the earth.

He didn't want anything, at least insofar as I knew. He was a senior in high school when I began my first year. He was a beautiful, graceful animal, a king of our forest, and everyone paid him homage.

My breathing came hard in his presence. I had to look away from the direct gaze of his eyes. His body scent made me feel intoxicated.

I seemed to amuse him. He toyed with me, seemingly unaware of how I flirted with him; how my face burned when he was near.

My longing for his body was enough to make me lose my senses. Yet I just kept smiling and talking, never telling him.

# PERSON AND PERSONA

In the years of my youth the affliction of loneliness was the scourge of my life.

Years ago during a visit to Vienna, I met a sensitive, attractive young American. I felt an intense need to make love. We were safely away from home in a foreign setting. He approached me with a veiled offer of what promised to be an ardent and fulfilling relationship if I would take merely a brief initiative.

I shied away. I could not have stood emotionally either taking such initiative or finding myself engaged with another man in the naked give-and-take of open sexuality. I had established a total separation between my person and the persona of a young man-of-God.

Anyone attempting to bridge that separation might be in for far more danger than he could possibly imagine.

# COURTED

What was his interest in me? I never understood. He was married, had two young daughters whom he loved, and was a busy executive with one of America's biggest corporations.

Yet he telephoned me—from San Francisco, Minneapolis, Chicago, Dallas; he wrote me letters; when he was in the New York area, where he lived with his family, he took me to dinner at the most expensive restaurants.

He never indicated by a touch, a look, a word, that he was attracted to me in a sexual or erotic way. He was always happy, secure, smiling, and absolutely aloof in intimate relations.

Once when he took me out to dinner, I couldn't help but notice that the tip he gave the man who parked his car was more than I was able, as a graduate student, to spend on food in two or three days.

He was handsome, but did not excite me at all. What I found interesting about him was that he actually courted me; listened endlessly to my problems, woes and petty triumphs; made me the center of his life when he was with me, and never spoke about his own life—including his absences from his wife when he was in my company.

I can't remember exactly how I heard of his sudden, unexpected death during a business trip that he made to San Francisco.

# LITERATI

I flew to the city for a cocktail party to launch a new book written by a friend of mine.

My hosts said to bring an overnight bag, and they would arrange a place for me to stay.

The party held in a townhouse was a brilliant success. Everyone seemed to have great fun. I drank too much but it didn't matter; energy burned off the alcohol immediately. Much later, someone came up to me and said I was spending the night at his place and he was glad to have me as his guest. He was darkly handsome and, I learned, a writer-editor.

When we left the party he carried my overnight bag to his car. We drove to his house. Which of two empty bedrooms did I want to sleep in, he asked. I said it didn't matter; he should choose.

But first, he lit a fire in the grate of the living room, poured brandy, and we talked. When he reached out to touch my stockinged foot with his fingers, I felt happy.

In a few moments we lay together on a rug before the fire. Later, he selected the room in which we slept.

# THE NIGHT

The formality of the party was completely gone. There was no general outline to the ritual, which broke into little pieces.

But I had caught the compelling invitation in his eyes. He was a priest, and told me that I was always welcome to stay with him.

Several nights later, I did.

There was no sleep for us, except to doze restlessly between long periods of lust. He was dark and hairy, a man consumed by desire. I did not want the night to end. But finally, the sky lightened outside the window.

A few months later, I learned that the highly creative and beloved priest of a growing parish had been discovered to be a homosexual, and was dismissed from his post. He became a college professor.

# LIQUID EYES

He told me that he looked directly at the sun in order to make his eyes appear liquid, and recommended that I do the same.

I was crazy about him. He was Argentinean. We were in graduate school together in Switzerland, later at Oxford.

We went for long walks into a Swiss village to drink Beaujolais and talk enthusiastically about the elaborate plans we envisioned for our futures.

At Oxford, he said one night that he was horny and wished to visit a whore house. Would I accompany him? But all I wanted to do was embrace him, kiss him, take him to my bed. Yet I did not say so.

I shared virtually everything with him except my gayness, the central mystery at the core of my existence.

# TRYST

I was speaking to a New York audience. I saw his face.
Everything else was suddenly blotted out.

Would I be able to meet him? Or, would he become lost in
the large crowd and simply disappear from my life?

Afterward at a small reception, *there* he stood within a few
feet. Everyone else came up to shake my hand as the guest of
honor. He kept his distance. Then without warning, he was
at my side. He handed me a card that contained his name,
address and phone number. Could he see me one night that
week? Yes, I replied.

Our tryst was almost choreographed to be romantic. His
apartment was, in my eyes, a garret out of *La Boheme*. He was
extremely young, boyish, vulnerable, but not innocent.

When I walked away from his place the next morning, I
felt that it was spring. My walk was balletic, my spirit
refreshed, my self youthful.

On another occasion we met again. The second time went
awry. Romance was swept away; a complex mood of confused
motives and misunderstanding undid us. It was our fate to
enjoy a simple tryst, and let it go.

# PATRICIAN

The train was about to pull into the station. I heard its whistle blow as I stood on the platform, my bag at my side. I would shortly be on my way.

I had just visited a suburban church to be the guest preacher and assist at mass at its Sunday services. The priest was coolly patrician. He assumed that I would stay over and sleep with him. My occasional sex was likely as not to be with another priest, and I did not disappoint him. But the priest was a sad prisoner of some enclosed avenue, locked deep inside an outer role that he played.

After sex, he did not want to be touched. I lay beside him in bed, feeling caught in a tight vise of intolerable loneliness.

The next morning the priest and I stood on the suburban railway platform waiting for my train. We resembled two tragic figures in an artistic portrayal of alienation by Münch. A quiet parting was exchanged. Then, rain streaked the dirty window of the compartment in which I sat.

Later, when I was back inside my solitary room at the seminary, I missed the curiously aloof and sad priest. I wished that I could bring a warmth to his life and body, kindle his feelings, make him glow in the happy warmth of full love.

# ENERGY

It was a brilliant, sharp, biting, alert autumn morning. The harsh wind would soon be blowing snow. Leaves rested in great heaps on street corners and in yards.

Visiting the city to make a speech the next day before an audience of several thousand people, I felt depleted and melancholy, totally without energy.

That night I left my hotel room and went out for a walk. The streets were virtually empty. But when I stopped to look into a lighted store window, a well-dressed older man also stopped. We talked, laughed, and were at ease.

He accompanied me back to my hotel room. He told me that he sold men's clothes in a department store. I shared my anxiety about the next day's speech. We slept together that night, offering each other emotional security, making the warmest love.

In the morning he was dressed in his usual sartorial high style. After we ate hot croissants and drank coffee in the dining room of the hotel, he went off to his department store. I departed, happy and confident with my energy restored, to greet the thousands.

# THE EYES OF A POET

A romantic church organist placed his warm, experienced, loving mouth on my hungry phallus.

I moaned and cried out, holding onto his firm neck and naked shoulders. One of his fingers caressed a nipple that responded as if it were attached to a solar system of sensual delight. Enveloping my phallus, he brought it under steady control, while he never stopped the rhythmic lovemaking of his mouth, the insatiable caressing of his tongue.

Soon I came inexorably toward my first climax of utter joy. I flooded his mouth and throat with love juice, my sperm, the essence of my being that I gratefully wanted him to drink as a gift of nectar.

He was both passionate and gentle. I adored him, but he said that his lover would not approve if we saw each other again.

Many years later I had dinner with him in a restaurant on the upper west side of New York. But he was distant from me now, a dim, romantic figure, almost as if he looked out at me from inside a period daguerrotype.

Yet I would have come to him in an instant.

# THE GRAPE VINES

He was in love with me, and I was too stupid and naive to understand it.

We drove to the Napa Valley from San Francisco. We visited wineries most of the afternoon. Now, it was growing late.

Sensing that the time remaining in our day was nearly over, we walked through fields where the grapes grew on vines.

The setting sun cast shadows on the earth. The vines were heavy with grapes. Our sense of each other suddenly overwhelmed us both. We fell to the ground and rolled in the furrowed soil.

# WINTER

# OLDER BROTHER, YOUNGER BROTHER

I walked furiously through city streets late at night. The swiftly falling snow nearly blinded me. My face, hands and feet were freezing cold.

The stone canyons mocked my loneliness. A distant lighted window surely belonged to another planet, one where there was compassion and warmth.

I turned into a corner bar in the Village. A sense of electric excitement filled my body when I realized it was filled with men, and was gay.

A young man with dark hair and laughing, mocking eyes approached me. He said that he recognized me from having seen my photograph on book jackets. He was direct in his invitation to go home with him, as I was equally direct in accepting.

At his apartment, we made the most passionate love during the night. Afterward we saw each other on many different occasions. I thought that I was in love with him. He also believed that he loved me.

I *wanted* very much to be in love with him. We talked about making a life together. He fantasized us in the roles of an older and a younger brother, he being the latter and quite submissive. He told me of his sado-masochistic desires. Ours was an intense, neurotic, immensely satisfying relationship on an erotic basis.

Yet we held widely differing views on too many other subjects in order to have any kind of lasting peace.

# WRESTLING

Outside the house lay the first snowfall of the season. I heard its curious stillness, as definitive a sound as thunder.

Then I raced outside to walk through soft drifts and make first tracks in the freshly fallen snow.

I had stayed all night in the house with its Armenian owner. He was a myriad of men all in one. His moods ran the full spectrum of human possibility. He was alternately warm and generous, then jealous and argumentative.

Feeling that he wanted to possess my soul as well as my body, I resisted with all my might this ultimate assault on my freedom.

However, he was boyish as well as macho, and could scarcely be denied. We eschewed his bed, and lay on the floor of his house, wrestling furiously in love.

# HEAD TABLE

I visited Houston, that energetic giant among cities. It was a glamorous visit accompanied by many parties, elaborate dinners and famous people.

However, I realized that I was alone, and wished to correct the fact. But, how? Invited to yet another fashionable party, I arrived early. I saw him seated at the bar. Joining him there, I said that I felt like having a margarita. Did this bar make a good one?

Tolerably good, he said, although he knew how to make one better. I ordered a margarita, sipped it, and commented that I had had better.

Oh?, he asked. Yes, I said.

We went to his apartment where he made me a margarita. It was much better than the one at the bar.

We got into his bed. Yet I was due shortly at the head table of a prominent dinner party where I was to speak.

Our loving exchangè transcended mere time, but we also met the demands of the clock. Just when the dinner party commenced, I was seated properly at the head table, my hair neatly combed, my smile positively euphoric.

# THE ARMY OFFICER

I was working at my first job in Hollywood as a producer at an ad agency, in charge of a network radio program.

On weekends I often saw a young woman who had been in college with me, and whose family owned a large house in Los Angeles. A crowd always went boating from there, drank and ate well, and I was given a blanket invitation to join them.

I met him one weekend at their home. He was an army officer stationed nearby. He was a glorious cliché—with a face that launched a thousand ships, an infectious smile, an easy presence, an all-American body; and he liked me very much.

Saturdays we went out on the boat with other guests, lay on the deck in the sun, drank beer, laughed, and found life easy. Saturday nights we shared a bed in the family home— and never touched. How I managed to avoid it, I don't know. I was in love with him.

Sundays we lazed around, drank coffee, ate Eggs Benedict, read the papers, yawned, dozed, dreamed—and finally he went back to the Army while I prepared to go back the next morning to my ad agency.

One day the Army gave him orders. After he departed, I never heard of him again.

# SHARING

As we lay sharing his double bed, he told me about his ideal mate.

My companion was a young priest, closeted, hurt, threatened. He had reached out in his search for love and sexual expression, and fallen in love with a man who did not respond to him.

The priest was someone who indubitably made it difficult to understand him. He properly wore his symbolic black clerical suit and white collar, played his role of an assured administrator and counselor, but underneath the trappings was someone quite different—insecure, lonely, anxious, and confused about where to go in his life.

He had become a jokester in public, someone who laughs fairly constantly and loudly as a means of diverting attention from his inner pain and conflict. As he lay naked next to me in bed, he was an utter stranger to his cultivated public image.

He and I were much apart in terms of love-sex experiences and expectations, yet still shared basic needs. Sensing this, I satisfied and comforted him directly and happily. He did the same for me.

In the morning he made us coffee. We talked honestly about what both of us sought in our lovers.

# CANUTE

Was it his shyness that attracted me to him? Or, maybe it was the curious mix of the devilish and the angelic in his easy smile.

I met him in a gay bar in Denver in the late '50s. It wasn't very gay because there were implicit threats of police harassment or arrest, and blackmail, in making the public disclosure that one was homosexual by appearing in the bar.

Merman and Garland played on the jukebox. I nervously sipped a watered-down scotch. We made contact. We went to my motel room. Shortly, we found that we were deliriously happy in each other's company.

Every Friday night I met him in the bar. He stayed with me until the next Saturday afternoon, when I must drive back alone to the small Colorado town in which I lived a closeted existence as a priest.

He earned his living as a short-order cook and a waiter. We were uninhibited in our free play, innocents who defied all the odds and claimed a small stake of pure happiness. But, it was doomed. There was no support system for our transitory relationship that was limited to an existence twenty-four hours a week inside a curtained motel room. There, we hid, loved, and earnestly tried to shut out the rest of the world.

Like King Canute trying to hold back the waves, we failed.

# IN THE GYM

I was taking a shower in the university gymnasium after a swim in the pool.

He stood next to me, also taking a shower. I knew him slightly. He was a professor. He looked carefully at my body and said that I appeared to be in wonderful shape. I laughed and agreed with him. I thought nothing more of our meeting.

Several weeks afterward, we found ourselves at the same faculty lunch and sat next to each other. He acted strangely and seemed to be out of control. His words directed to me were sexually explicit. He placed his hand upon my leg and kept it there. But we were in public, in the company of others, and also in a most conservative setting that would not accept out-of-the-ordinary behavior.

The others seemed not to notice anything amiss. I tried to reason with him very quietly, telling him that we would meet later and talk honestly about ourselves. It seemed to have very little effect upon him. Apparently he was consumed by frustrations and desires inside himself, and at this moment they spilled over his discretion and reserve.

I did not see him again. I heard a few days later that he and his wife had abruptly left the university for the rest of the year because of a sudden illness.

# TACITURN

The weather was freezing cold. It was after dark when I arrived at his place, having driven in my car most of the day to get there.

His was a rural church out on the plains. He lived next door to it in a small frame house.

A taciturn young priest, he was seemingly tied in knots emotionally. He was cold as ice. His laconic manner spurred my feeling of necessity to start a conversation. However, I found myself giving a monologue.

We ate dinner which he had prepared. The food was sparse and the silence bleak. I yearned to get to bed as a way of simply being alone, putting an end to unpleasantness. The next morning I would preach the guest sermon in his church and be on my way.

I was startled when he said there was only one bed and we would share it. When we undressed, I noticed the pure whiteness of his naked muscular body.

One side of the bed was placed against the wall. He asked me to climb into bed first, and occupy the side against the wall, so that he could get up first in the morning to start a fire.

After I climbed into bed, he turned off the light and followed me. The sheets were bitter cold. However, his body was warmer than a fire when he took me in his arms.

# THE NOTEBOOK

I placed my hand on the cold airplane window and looked outside. There was only a swirling sort of infinity for me to see, low clouds and falling snow.

I was on a book promotion tour. A dozen interviews awaited me in Chicago during the next two days. Television, radio and press reporters would ask every conceivable question about my new book.

A very professional looking young man, clad in a suit and wearing glasses, met my plane. He worked for the publisher, and drove me to the hotel. After I checked-in, he asked if I would like to have dinner with him. It would be a delight not to have to eat alone. We went up to my room and he waited while I took a quick shower and dressed.

After we dined, he took me to an artists' hangout for a glass of wine. We sat on cushions in a candlelit room, and talked. Realizing that the time was getting late, with interviews to do the next day, I said that I really should be getting back to the hotel. On the way, he talked about publishing. He was so serious. I wondered what lay beneath the veneer.

However, as he let me out at the hotel entrance, he suddenly discovered that he must have left his notebook in my room. Did I mind if he came up with me to get it?

When he took off his glasses and got out of his suit, his professional facade vanished. I found him to be a warm, wise, lively, refreshing, loving man.

# ON A PEDESTAL

I guess that I gave him the image he wanted in the company of a young, newly-ordained priest.

He was gay, closeted and Anglo-Catholic. He channeled most of his energy into church work, and was also an organist.

We often dined in his tiny apartment. The air was stale, for he refused to open his windows. He gave me attention, time, food and adoration; virtually everything but love and sexual release.

He went to bars and baths for sex; he considered it a dirty necessity, and then went to confession to be absolved before his next visit to more baths and bars.

Alone on a pedestal, I masturbated.

# THE BISHOP

The Bishop was an elegant man. His bearing was military, body neat, manners impeccable.

He and I were among ten guests who had been invited to lunch.

The Bishop, whom I had met only once before, and I were both out-of-town visitors.

Cocktails preceded lunch. The Bishop and I sipped diabolically dry Martinis. After chatting over our cocktails in a marvelously decorated room that had a high-beamed ceiling and a great fireplace with a crackling fire, we moved into the dining room.

The Bishop and I were seated next to one another at the table.

"I liked your last book more than anything else you've written," he said, and smiled warmly at me.

I thanked him. Such a remark can be a bit of a cliché in my experience. I wondered if he had read the book. The table conversation ebbed and flowed, never intent on going very far.

After a dessert of trifle, followed by coffee, the luncheon guests moved back into the room with the fire. Brandy was served. The Bishop laid his hand on my shoulder. He said that he needed to have a brief conversation with me in private. He had mentioned this to our host, who told the Bishop that we could chat in an upstairs bedroom. Would I please accompany him there? Certainly, I replied.

Our footsteps sounded like those of choirboys as they hit the wooden stairs. When we had climbed to the second floor, the Bishop directed me toward a room whose door stood open.

After we walked inside the room, he closed the door. He looked at me, and now the warmth of his eyes disappeared.

"Take off all your clothes," the Bishop abruptly told me.

I looked at him in shock and disbelief. But the coldness of his demeanor underscored his words. To be quite honest, I looked upon any Bishop at that time as something of a god-figure. I also experienced an inexplicable feeling of being consumed by wonderment and teased by fear.

Slowly, I removed my jacket, got my tie off, then my shirt. His look revealed sternness and determination. Feeling a fool stripping before the Bishop's eyes, without asking him why or attempting to hold a conversation, I opened my belt, pulled down the zipper, and climbed out of my pants. Then I dropped my shorts.

Still, there was no communication from him. I bent over, untied my shoes and removed them, then pulled off my socks. I stood before the Bishop stark naked.

"Lay face down on the bed," he told me. I did so, feeling the titillation of a half erection. Nothing quite like this had ever happened to me before and I was unprepared for whatever was to follow. Surely, I reasoned, the Bishop had no idea that I was gay.

The Bishop's right hand moved slowly over my buttocks, then up and down my legs.

"If you haven't been a good boy, I will have to whip your bare ass," he said.

The heavy, cold episcopal ring on his hand lay on my naked ass as if it were an instrument of possible torture.

"Do you ever entertain impure thoughts, or touch yourself on the lower parts of your body, or masturbate?" he asked. "If so, I must whip you."

I didn't breathe. What did he expect me to say? Would he actually whip me if my answer displeased him? What else might take place in this room with the Bishop? But, surely, we should quickly rejoin the other guests downstairs who must be beginning to wonder what we were doing.

"Bishop," I said hoarsely, "I have tried very hard to be a good boy."

The Bishop held his hand on my naked buttocks. Time stopped for me inside the room. Suddenly, I heard the clear ticking of a grandfather clock somewhere else on the second floor of the house.

"All right," the Bishop said. But his hand stayed on my warm buttocks. As I lay face down on the bed, beneath his figure clothed in black, I was as horny as I had ever been in my life. My face felt flushed and my breathing was strained.

Finally, the Bishop broke the long silence.

"This time you can go," he said. "But you had better make sure that you are a good boy. If you are not—and don't think I won't know about it—I shall have to whip your bare bottom the next time."

Standing up, I dressed as quickly as I could. Not another word was said. We left the room and walked downstairs to rejoin the other guests in front of the crackling fire.

The Bishop wore his handsome pectoral cross and a serene smile.

# GOLDEN HAIR

His fey expression and golden hair made him resemble a wondrous figure in a panel of medieval stained-glass.

His smile was elfin. A young Irish priest, his manner was marked by a strange sort of enchantment and mischievousness. Whenever I found him in an occasional uncharacteristic dour mood, all I had to do was speak gently, and gaze tenderly into his momentarily intractable eyes. In a flash, the fog of his nature would clear, the clouds disappear, and he smiled back at me from an illuminated expression.

I could not imagine living an earthly existence with such a creature from another world. However, I was delighted to be with him for a short time.

During a walk one afternoon we stopped to examine a stream alongside our path. A leaf which had been captured there inside winter ice was now free, a part of the springtime's running stream.

I never told him that I loved him except with my eyes and by my actions.

# TEDDY BEAR

Am I the only one who has known the fear that there will be no solid ground when I need it most?

I had felt depressed for days. Now, visiting New Orleans in the winter when it was raining, my spirits did not lift. The French Quarter seemed about to drown, a streetcar named desire led nowhere, and the most sensuous food and drink simply bored me.

At my moment of lowest ebb, I was seated next to him at a dinner party.

He fit none of my descriptions of the right fantasy figure, for he was over-weight, slightly Santa Claus-like, and his face was jowly. But he was charming beyond measure, his smile would melt ice, his voice was hypnotic, and his touch was mesmerizing.

When I lay inside his arms in bed, I found that his hairy body was more welcome than a warm cave in a cold forest. He looked more macho than Richard the Lion-Hearted, yet he was gentler than spring rain.

# THE YOUNG MAN (I)

I came to know a theatre director, an older man fallen on bad days and going downhill in his career. His need of love was desperate. But I was selfish, caught in a vision of my youthful beauty.

Late one morning we were alone in his apartment. It was crowded with memorabilia of his lifetime devoted to the stage. The director expected that we would make love. He was a good person. Surely I was as much in need of relationship and sexual release as he was. However, when I saw his face come close to mine, I reacted in terror.

His face looked so old.

Did I think that I saw death there? Why couldn't I see him instead of succumbing to the youth cult's fiat against age, shutting out his nobility and need? His mouth opened to kiss me. I saw a forbidding cave, an abyss of horror. I cried out. I beat against his body with my fists. I hid my face from the director, pleading with him to let me go quickly without explanation, and try to understand that I couldn't help but act this way.

Gently, the director got my coat, helped me into it, and showed me to the door. He asked me to call when I was able. I never called.

# THE YOUNG MAN (II)

Years later I went dancing with a young man.

I liked him. At the end of the evening I asked the man if he wanted to spend the night with me.

I felt very lonely, and believed I had a lot of energy and love to share. But the young man said no. He explained that he had to get to work early the next morning, and should start home and go to bed alone.

I studied his face for a long moment. I looked for clues. Yet it's possible that the answer was simple. Had the entire situation simply come full circle?

I had to laugh, mostly at myself.

# PEACE AND QUIET

Two friends had invited me to stay with them. When I accepted I did not realize one of them was a candidate in the throes of a hotly contested local political campaign.

Loud meetings never ended before 3 a.m. in the room adjoining the one in which I tried to sleep. Vainly counting sheep, I heard emotional outbursts and dark rumblings of ideological bickering. The telephone rang so constantly that the cat got sick and started to vomit. What could I do? The house was an historic manse, the food exquisite, the drink nectar, but I was losing my mind.

When my friends invited a graduate law student who lived nearby to join us for dinner, I realized he might afford me the sole available parachute for survival. Could he put me up for the night at his place, I asked. Glad to, he replied.

All that I sought was peace and quiet, but I found neither. Although the student and I were different in almost every way as to boggle the mind, our chemistry and stars were radiantly on target. Reaching his apartment, we simply fell into each other's arms and made uncomplicated, long, sensuous, rewarding love for the rest of the night.

And the night after that.

Malcolm Boyd & John Due
Photo © 1980 Roger Ressmeyer

# EPILOGUE

# OUR LOVE

When I first met you, my feelings ran deeper from the very beginning than I was prepared to admit to myself. You delighted me.

Your piercing eyes that held my gaze and wouldn't look away. The Prince Valiant haircut. Your broad shoulders, the start of a pot belly unless you dieted, firm round buns. Your tender mouth.

Our love for one another grew in the ensuing weeks and months. You always said it wasn't my body that turned you on so much as my total personality. I had also not initially been turned on solely by your body, although I liked it very much; rather, I responded to you as a whole person who fascinated me. I loved your laugh, candor and utter absence of phoniness, your intensity, forthrightness, ready sense of humor, and boundless energy.

# HOLIDAY

We took a holiday in San Francisco. Our hotel window looked out upon a bank.

Five mornings a week, a banker sat at a desk in his office whose window afforded him a box seat to look into our room. Often we made love while the banker sat facing us, but he never looked up from his work. Apparently he never saw us, as he concentrated instead on the pressing business that was piled high on his desk.

Do you remember how we talked about him and tried to figure him out? He arrived at work extremely early (his presence punctuated our lovemaking) and departed quite late. Did he commute from a distant suburb, we wondered. Was he happy. Had his wife taken a lover because of neglect and boredom. Had he sold only his body to the bank, or his soul, too?

One day you and I drove to the wine country north of San Francisco. At St. Helena we tasted whites and reds and rosés at Beaulieu, Louis Martini, Charles Krug, Christian Brothers, Beringer, Inglenook and Mondavi. We felt positively euphoric after the samples of Cabernet Sauvignon, Johannisberg Riesling, Zinfandel, Pinot Chardonnay and the rest. How romantic. What joy. Our near-fatal mistake came when we ordered wine with our dinner in a resaturant that night, for we were already adrift on a Grecian sea of vino. But later in our motel room, you achieved the greatest peak of sexual fulfillment that you had yet known with me. Abashed and delighted, I believed that I enjoyed it even more than you did.

# PING PONG

I was born in Manhattan and felt at home there. You, on the other hand, looked upon San Francisco as your ideal city. You had often been in New York but, like many visitors there, had found the pace maddening, people unyielding, and manners inexplicable.

We shared a visit to New York when one of my books was published, and attended a cocktail party thrown by my publisher in honor of the new tome. You wore your new corduroy suit. Your hair looked splendid. You seemed to be relaxed. But I was a cat on a hot tin roof, noting what invited guests were not in attendance, checking the status of critics who were there, and swiftly deciding the event was a disaster that would make the crash of the Titanic resemble a Shirley Temple flick.

While I was busy as a ping pong ball bouncing up to greet each new guest, you and a man from *Time* got locked into heavy, heavy conversation. A well-known writer sided up to me and, having downed her fourth Martini, said: "Darling, this is really your best book. I'm so proud of you, baby. Ungh-h-h-h!" Utter bullshit, I thought. Where *were* you, I wondered. How much longer did we have to stay?

# IN ORBIT

A second party that same evening awaited you and me. It was an annual bash given by my literary agent.

We were tired. Our nerves were taut. Too many things were happening to us, and we seemed to be in orbit. We began to argue. Our dispute was not a rational one. I felt that I had suffered enough during the long hidden years of being, first, a queer and, later, a homosexual. Now, I was gay, and determined to be *gay*. The pathology of the homosexual experience was something that I was adamant about consigning permanently to the junk heap.

"I've paid my dues," I said when we were back in our hotel room. "Now I want to be happy. I'm going to be happy. There won't be any more bullshit in my life."

You were shouting contrapuntally at me. I couldn't hear what you were saying. I only saw your angry face. I felt that I was in dead center of the worst nightmare in the world.

# THIS STRANGER WHOM I LOVE

I struck you. Both of us fought with our fists. Later, shouting, we lay on the floor of the room and wrestled. Finally we were exhausted.

Somehow, we stopped shouting and fighting and got into bed. We had agreed long ago never to sleep in separate beds away from one another. Now, too, we slept in the same bed, as if by some reflex action.

Exhausted, we fell asleep right away. I awoke sometime in the middle of the night. I gazed at your naked body lying beside me. Who is this stranger whom I love, I wondered. How can I live without him. But I can't live with him. It's hopeless, the whole thing. Apparently I don't know him at all.

But you no longer resembled a monster with tongues of fire streaking out of your mouth. You looked very tender and likable. I wanted to kiss you. I desired more than anything to take your sleeping body into my arms and love you.

However, how could I do this if I were leaving you in the morning? I sighed. Shortly I fell asleep again.

When I awakened in the morning, I heard you brushing your teeth in the bathroom. A moment later I was beside you, and we embraced. We made a decision to stay together. We would find a way through our problems.

# NEW YEAR'S EVE

At noon we had lunch at Sutter's Mill. The place was packed.

That afternoon you and I wandered through the stone canyons of San Francisco's financial district as ticker tape cascaded from open windows to the streets below. We filled our arms with tape, carried it back to our Castro apartment, and threw it out the window after dark. In the evening we went dancing at a disco. But we found the crowds distracting and boring. Soon we retreated to our home and happily held one another in bed when the sounds of midnight hit like an earthquake.

The next morning we did what we had planned to do for fun. We sat in a movie theater for the day's first showing of *King Kong*. In our great happiness, it looked like a combination of *Gone With the Wind* and *Citizen Kane*. But while we were inside the theater, rain had begun to fall. Our long walk back to our home in the pouring rain left us soaked to the skin. The aftermath was inescapable pure romance.

# A SANDCASTLE

It was a beautiful time and a bittersweet one, happy and unhappy, tender and harsh, civilized and wild, impractical and pragmatic, cruel and caring, intensely human. Finally, I have come to feel deeply fulfilled, peaceful and secure in our relationship.

Memories. So many of mine will always include you. Our years together—turbulent, funny, touching, never dull. Your crackling rage at the time of a full moon; and your otherwise unending, never failing grace and sense of humor.

If someone asked me to describe you in a single frame, what would I say? Would it be one of lovemaking as I held you? A frame of you laughing or crying, angry or peacefully content? None of these.

It is a picture of you at the seashore—I wading out into the water, but turning to watch—making a sandcastle.

# MALCOLM BOYD
# AN INTERVIEW

MALCOLM BOYD was born June 8, 1923 in New York. In the 1940s he worked in Hollywood and New York as a partner of Mary Pickford in P.R.B., Inc., a pioneer TV production company. He was first president of the Television Producers Assn. of Hollywood.

In the 1950s Malcolm Boyd entered an Episcopal seminary. He was ordained a priest. *The New York Times Magazine* has described him as "A latter-day Luther or a more worldly Wesley, trying to move organized religion out of 'ghettoized' churches into the streets—where the people are."

In the 1960s Malcolm Boyd became a leader in the civil rights and peace movements. His best-selling book *Are You Running With Me, Jesus?* was published. He made international headlines when he appeared for a month in San Francisco's hungry i. . . . He became an Associate Fellow at Yale. . . . One of the "Red-Hot 100" in "The Take-Over Generation," *Life* cover story. . . . A "Disturber of the Peace" (with Federico Fellini, Norman Mailer, James Baldwin, Jules Feiffer and William F. Buckley, Jr.) *Mademoiselle.* . . . He spoke on more than 100 campuses including Harvard, Michigan, Stanford, M.I.T., Cornell, Columbia and Vassar. . . . " Not only has he been 'where the action is,' he has, in fact, often been the action."—*Philadelphia Bulletin.*

In the 1970s Malcolm Boyd was honored as an author when he was invited to live in Jerusalem for three months as a guest of Mishkenot Sha'ananim, the centre for artists and writers. He has written 19 books [including two autobiographical works, *As I Live and Breathe,* Random House, 1970 and *Take Off the Masks,* Doubleday, 1978] and edited two others. . . . He received the Herzl Award for service to the Jewish people. . . . He joined Chief Justice Warren Burger, Lord Chief Justice Widgery of England and other distinguished leaders as a principal speaker at the "Bicentennial of American Law" at the New York University School of Law in 1976. . . . Boston University established The Malcolm Boyd Collection, a permanent archive of his letters and papers. . . . *People* magazine (Sept. 27, 1976) described him as "blunt, restless, eloquent and above all, open"; yet it noted: "He has kept one aspect of his life deeply private: his homosexuality." He had just announced that he is gay. . . . The best-selling *Book of Lists* included him in its list of "67 renowned homosexuals and bisexuals" throughout history.

The present interview was taped in New York City by Edward Curtin, Jr. It appeared originally in *Gay Sunshine Journal* 44/45—10th Anniversary Issue (1980).

EDWARD CURTIN: *It's been about two years now since you 'came out of the closet.' I'm wondering if you're glad, after the experiences of the past two years, that you did?*

MALCOLM BOYD: It's been an incredible experience. And probably very few people would be able to understand all the complexities and nuances of it. I wouldn't have missed coming out for the world. Honesty required it. What else can I say? I think for anyone to be living lies or in shadows or wearing masks any more than is absolutely necessary is anti-human and anti-God and a travesty; there aren't even words for it. So it's more than liberating, there's a lot of very deep theology connected with it. I still think that I feel more than anything else like the character played by Jack Nicholson in the Antonioni film, *The Passenger*, where someone has died of a heart attack and someone else looks like him, and the other person takes his passport and clothes and his identity and his life. (laughs) Because I don't think there's anyone who doesn't respond to my coming out quite differently.

*I remember that you wrote in your book,* Take off the Masks, *that when you were first considering going public you were warned that doing so would ruin your 'effectiveness' and would lead to your 'crucifixion'. Has this happened?*

I don't know if I can answer that. It would depend on how one would define 'crucifixion' and 'effectiveness'. It has ironically brought me closer to what I would call the way of the Cross than anything that ever happened before in my life. I feel very privileged, but in fact, it's hard to talk about that. I don't wish to sound arrogant, and it *is* a very private thing, but on the other hand, I'm not a private person. But that experience is very similar to it; it's almost a heady experience in a sense. One is living one's own death, and one, in a certain sense, i in tune with life; the perspective on everything is altered. I look at things quite differently now—certainly success and failure—but all the lines and shadows are coming together. And I could talk for an hour on the effectiveness question, but I don't know what it would prove.

*What have been the problems that you've encountered since you 'came out' and how do these problems compare to those you encountered before?*

Well, they're qualitatively different, but I smiled when you asked the question because in a sense, there's been nothing but problems; on the other hand, there was nothing but problems before. (laughs) And I see life as a struggle and a pilgrimage anyhow, so I have no nirvana picture of picking a safe place in an imaginary sunbelt and having no problems. That would be the most hideous thing I could think of. The problems, I suppose, have been with virtually everybody in my life and everyone I meet. I'm a little like Ellison's 'Invisible Man', except that I'm visible, but in essence, the experience is what Ellison is writing about, being a figment of people's imagination. Sexuality, I have learned, touches the deepest nerve in our society. And we live a ritualized lie in terms of sexuality. I knew the ground rules; I grew up with the ritual. I didn't know what it meant to move against the ritual until now. It is the most subversive thing, apparently, that one can do. And most people prefer putting it on a wrestling-with-shadows situation. They prefer not to have a confrontation, not to deal with controversy, and to put you in Coventry or to say that you don't exist or the book doesn't exist—this kind of thing. But with close friends, there's been a lot of agonizing on their parts, and I'm aware of that. Not only am I not sorry, I'm grateful, because I think it's contributed to all of our growth. And this has been essential for everybody who's been involved with me. And it's by no means over. Before, you see, I was just slowly committing suicide and I was going along on one or two cylinders. I was denying my life, my courage; I painted myself into a corner, and there was just a little point left where my feet were. And I took a mighty leap across that room, and there was a door, and it opened.

*Would you say that the need to deny your life—anyone's need to deny his other life—is built into the Christian view of reality?*

I think it's anti-Christian, but I think it's culturally Christian. I saw Massenet's opera, *Werther,* and one saw again, as in Ibsen's *A Doll's House,* a social structure in which people were choreographed. I think that a cultural takeover of Christianity, a cultural use of Christianity for its own ends, has included not only a so-called Christian blessing on national war, but a cultural use of sexual energy so that people are choreographed into a certain pattern that, for example, benefited capitalism, to say the least. Hopefully contained sexual energies—hopefully, that is, in terms of the state's wishes—reinforced role playing, allowed certain outlets for pent-up sexual energy if one played this by the ground rules and was sophisticated enough to know what one was doing and how. And the irony was to put the imprimatur of Christ on this madness. And I think the crisis of Christendom in western civilization is that an increasingly growing number of people will have nothing further to do with this, and the Church is unable to be honest; it is unable to serve Christ, even to acknowledge Christ, because the Church has for so long been the handmaiden of the state. Caesaro-Papism in our culture at this moment would make anything in the Byzantine Empire look like kindergarten.

*To follow that up somewhat, isn't there an irreconcilable conflict between the affirmation of one's sexual/bodily life and death, as long as Christians believe in the duality between body and soul?*

Well, then Christians who claim to believe in the Resurrection don't believe in it at all, which is again one of the savage conflicts, and it's why Christendom is dying, because people are no longer content to put their time and energy into something that tells so fundamental a lie to them. The duality between body and soul is certainly built into the cultural/social framework of Christianity, as we have developed it in western civilization. The idea of the virgin birth seems similar to this. In other words, that Mary wasn't passionately and in a sweaty sexual, physical way in bed with Joseph, both as instruments of the Holy Spirit creating Jesus. But the implication is that Mary, in a very 'pure'—and I would certainly have to put that in quotes, because I don't believe in it—non-sexual, non-sweaty, nongenital way, without orgasm, created Jesus. I think if you accept the virgin birth and mean it, this leads to so many conflicts in one's life. The idea of Jesus as a sexless being, a celibate, I see no evidence of at all, nor do I see evidence of sexuality. I was just rereading Matthew, Mark, Luke and John in one fell swoop. It's interesting every so often to read the four of them together again and just get an overall view. It's very difficult in reading those four gospels to come down on one side or the other about a number of things about Jesus. And I don't really understand why. Healing, of course, takes up seemingly half of the gospels; healing is about totally ignored by the Church. And then when you get to Jesus, they deal with what he said, his parables and teachings and healings; they really don't deal with him when he went to bed or when he was having breakfast or . . . they're public, not private. Almost the only private thing, in a sense, seems to be

Gethsemane. So you can't look to the gospels for very much, at this level.

I assume, on the basis of Jesus being the most perfect being, of his having lived for thirty-three years on earth, incarnating God and the whole thing, sacrificing himself, I assume sensuousness and full sexuality. There are almost no guidelines in this; he certainly was in the company of men most of the time, but I think to say that that means he was gay or homosexual is somewhat absurd. You can't really come to any conclusion: bisexual, heterosexual. But you don't get an impression of a man without passion or profound humanity; you don't get any sense of some sort of prissy guy, hiding himself, standing around detached from human life, not at all. I don't get from him any duality of body and soul, and I have to come back to the importance of Jesus Christ in a much simpler way, as I approach Christianity. As a matter of fact, I think the Church's problem is that it has wandered so far away from Jesus Christ that it is simply unrecognizable. So I take a guidline from Jesus Christ on body and soul being together. To what extent I always knew this, even when I repressed or denied it, I cannot sit here and just say too clearly.

*Do you think that, like yourself, all gays should take off the masks?*

I would hope that it wouldn't be just gays who would take off the masks; I see this as a very masked society. There is the prayer, 'They're in a Golden World, Jesus', which is in *Are You Running with Me, Jesus?*, where everybody is wearing masks. I see something awfully sad in having to wear them. As to whether all gays should come out of the closet, this has to be up to individual gay people. And the timing has to be left up to an individual, and I don't think anyone can push too much, or should. No, I see no uniform rules at all. The diversity of gay life is, if anything, a little more than the diversity of 'ordinary' life.

*If a person, a gay person, 'came out of the closet' today, what would you say are the personal and social ramifications in doing so or in not doing so?*

It's a little like the advice I would give Jewish friends planning to move to Israel, because having lived in Israel, I'd say learn Hebrew before you go, not after, and also be aware that once you get to Jerusalem, you shouldn't write checks for gin or vodka on your American bank account; you'd better have your bank account there and live as other people do, or else stay in Kansas City. In other words, you're going to be entering a new terrain in coming out. And it's very important and interesting to understand that terrain. There'll be quite a lot of nakedness without masks; you'd better be prepared to deal with mother and father and brother and sister and others who are close to you. You know, you're really dealing with the nitty-gritty now, so you'd better know that before coming out. There can be economic ramifications, and you'd better understand that. Certainly, there will be a new freedom for you, but a number of us have understood the difference between freedom and license, I think, for some time. With freedom comes responsibility, so if you think that you're casting yokes to the wind and you're going to have some kind of mad fantasy freedom, you're not only wrong, but you've equated freedom with license. To come out of the closet is a socially responsible act, and you will have to act socially responsible in relationship to it. Which means you have a teaching role; you're a role model, whether you wish to be or not; you are a walking queer, faggot, homosexual, gay, or whatever you want to call it for an awful lot of people you may not wish to be that for. It will alter just about every part of your life. It's a very major decision, and I can't think of a counterpart to it because very few blacks in our society are passing as non-blacks, chicanos aren't passing, and women aren't going around dressed up as men and living as men and secretly going to the bathroom at General Motors. So I can't think of a counterpart for this role. Without experience, in other words, it's very difficult.

*What did you mean when you wrote that 'gay has something of universal meaning to say to everybody'?*

There are a couple of different points. For one, homosexuality for thousands of years has been the unnameable leprosy. And in almost all cultures, it's been freely regarded as reason for torture, torment and terrible things. It's just the unnameable dreadful thing. For anyone to reach a level of self-esteem where one is actually proud of oneself, including that part, and able to see everything as God's creation, is what I would call tremendous. The other point is that gay for a long time meant a kind of Noel Coward brittleness, a kind of upper-middle-class game. And everybody knew it, and as long as it was safely choreographed, it was acceptable if one was aristo-cratic and charming and paid one's dues. This meant that at the top level of society, homosexuality was able to exist according to ground rules. And gay then meant laughing to cover up one's tears. You know, somebody would either have a nice lunch with you at a nice French restaurant or a good pillow fight. I think gay now means, in a new context, an extraordinary openness, a cutting through levels of sham and hypocrisy, an actual sharing of oneself with other people. I think this has a great deal to say to everybody in an age where we have more masks and rituals and customs than the Ming Dynasty. If there were a Rip Van Winkle situation or some-one landed in our society out of a time capsule from another age, it might be very hard to survive more than fifteen minutes in terms of knowing the games we play.

*Do you think that masks should all be dropped and that lies that people tell to themselves and to each other, no matter how small, should be stopped?*

I'm not going to do a Savonarola because a lot of judgment could be called forth; that would be very dangerous. There's a pitfall there for a tremendous amount of self-righteousness that would be very dangerous. From a standpoint of ethics, when one doesn't tell the whole truth, the norm, as far as I'm concerned, should be love. Someone is dying, and out of love, one person would say to someone dying, 'You are dying', and out of love, someone else would not say it. It depends upon the people involved and other things that you and I sitting here cannot enumerate. To speak a kind of total truth about everything, this has to be weighed in terms of the vulnerability of people, their strengths. There's a lot of fragility involved that has to be considered. And I don't think for us the question is to go from here to there, meaning that you have to cross this bridge into a kind of situation where there's total, full honesty and you have to talk about everything. It's really more of a situation of wanting more honesty and more openness, and realizing that to cross a bridge and have it has a kind of Oz-like quality that's unreal. But the way we're able to do it in our own lives is to take a step at a time, and to do it relationship by relationship, because for a number of people in relationships now, if they wish to have a different degree of honesty, it would mean probably terminating the relationship and entering into a new one, because a relationship is two people, and the other person might not wish it. Of course, it has very complex ramifications from a pragmatic standpoint.

*You were very active in the civil rights movement. Can you or do you compare your experiences in the civil rights movement with your present experiences in the gay liberation movement?*

The big difference is that I was doing something for someone else in civil rights, and now, as a privileged white male, I find myself, ironically, in a minority of my own. I do see lots of connections between the movements. Also, don't forget there was the anti-war movement tucked in there somewhere, too. I can laugh at it with a looseness now. I'm no longer a self-righteous young zealot, thank God. For us to take anything totally seriously, including ourselves, is ridiculous. I can see the absurdity of all movements and establishments, and self-serving people without a sense of humor who think they've got to get the *New York Times* to print their publicity release and half the battle will be won. Or we don't want to compromise ourselves, but we do want a half million dollars from a very rich foundation. (laughs) So-and-so was a son-of-a-bitch, but was just shot to death, and so is now a martyr who will be honored forever and prayed over in a stained-glass window. One could go on. I think one of the most difficult things for me sometimes, in terms of any movement, is to meet someone very, very young and idealistic, who is just beginning to work and who might find what I just said shocking. In other words, we really aren't good guys and bad guys, and the people I might mistrust the most now are people who would sit here unblinkingly and without any humor, and insist they're the good guys.

*You would expect that in the case of your recent book,* Take Off the Masks, *that the 'good guys' who would at least review the book would be the liberal journals and newspapers in this country. Has that been the case?*

*Take Off the Masks* is the victim of an attempt to ignore it. In a curious sense, I guess that's backfired. You know, the book *is* finding its audience. I've received over a thousand letters. And one-third of them are sort of hateful attacks noting scripture, and two-thirds are letters that would break your heart or make you laugh in a very healthy way. From Roman Catholic priests, ministers of every stripe, and everybody else, gay and non-gay.

But we come now to a serious question about the media. Because I can remember when the media were anti-black. And an editor hearing or reading this might react with horror and disagreement, but he'd be wrong. I remember when the report of a black on the society page of a newspaper would have been unthinkable, in the same sense that I remember when blacks and whites couldn't get coffee together at a lunch counter. And I remember when responsible newspapers didn't have black journalists, and we would sweat out the reporting of the civil rights struggle, as I feel one sweats out the same thing with the gay struggle today. And I certainly remember the media with the question of the Vietnam war and how those of use who were demonstrating and struggling to bring the war to an end agonized about either having something not reported, or, as we felt, reported in the wrong perspective. And I think the response to *Take Off the Masks* is, in the larger sense, a response to gayness. And there are a number of people in the media who wish it would go away, or feel that they are locked into a kind of middle-class, liberal respectability where they cannot give credence to this. Or refuse to accept this as a part of the news. Or what—it's a mystery!

*Has the religious press ignored the book?*

I'd say at this point almost entirely. And *that* I didn't expect.

Because I'm an author of more than twenty books, and most of them have been reviewed in the pages of these journals. I've not been an unknown religious figure in this country. I've reviewed for many of the journals. I made news for them. It's incredible to watch them act as if the book didn't exist.

*Have any of them refused to take advertisements for your book?*

There are two publications which, according to my publisher, turned down the advertising copy, which was the same printed in the *New York Times Book Review*. And I think that those of us who are related to publishing at all know that the *New York Times Book Review* and *The New Yorker* are two publications that are very sensitive about copy. In other words, everything doesn't get in. And so you'd assume that something that had gotten into the *Times Book Review* would be perfectly okay for a mainline, major religious publication. I didn't get feedback from that. By that I mean I don't think my publisher went back and said, 'What in the copy do you object to? Might we make a change?' So what it meant to the book is that the amount of money that would have been spent in those two publications was added to the budget for the *New York Times Book Review* ad, which was simply larger. But it did deny me a kind of access in those religious publications. I have felt that the book has been denied access, which I find in a democratic situation, a free society, to be very threatening.

There are certain leading television programs that had me on many times before, but didn't this time. One such program, in Los Angeles, as a matter of fact, said that the viewers had communicated to the program director that they really now want no alternative lifestyles; they just want nuclear family input, and this would preclude me, as a gay person, speaking about this. That's why I'm astonished the book has been able to do as well as it has. I'm concerned not just about my book; I'm concerned about the dissemination of ideas in a free society. We ostensibly have a free press. Those of us who have been in underground situations for years know the establishment is reported routinely, and *we* have to 'make news' in order to be reported. This is why in civil rights and in the Vietnam war peace movement, the chicano movement, the women's liberation movement, and the gay movement, so many of us have, on a number of occasions, demonstrated and even been arrested because it required us to go and make that kind of sacrifice in order to get mentioned in the media, in terms not of an ego trip, but of our cause, so that people can at least have access to the ideas. Whereas establishment people are covered all the time as far as consecrations and inaugurations and marriages and all the rest of it. The *New York Times* is particularly faulty when claiming to tell the whole truth, in reporting the establishment, and either ignoring underground movements or making people get out of character or do things that get on the wire service.

*Do you think that the religious press is ignoring your book in the hope that you will go away and stop embarrassing them?*

I don't know. Obviously, I'm not going to go away. I have no wish to embarrass them. I think the Christian gospel embarrasses them, as I would hope it embarrasses all of us. It embarrasses me.

*You've written that 'sexual conformity has been propagated by rote' and 'that sexual liberation is a healthy and holy aspect of the human adventure.' Obviously, the issue we're discussing here today is not just homosexuality, but sexuality. What is your understanding of sexual liberation?*

Well, I'll take the negative as an illustration of the conformity end of what you asked. The young man was to sow his wild oats, so at least presumably he'd know what to do with his sexual equipment when he got in bed on the wedding night. It was also assumed that the young woman would not know what to do. In R. W. B. Lewis' biography of Edith Wharton, he writes of when she went to her mother before her wedding and she said she needed help in bed, and her mother said I can't offer you any help, you've seen statues—meaning men's genitalia. (laughs) And I remember the film, *The Emigrants,* with Liv Ullman, where the peasant man and woman are in bed, and they've worked hard all day. He needs sexual release; she says she can't stand another pregnancy, that she's been pregnant a number of times—because if he's going to have sexual release, it's going to automatically mean pregnancy. And you see them in bed together, and in a moment he rolls over, and obviously, they're going to have sex because they cannot sleep together in bed without having sex. Given the role of the male and female at that moment in society, his wishes will be honored. Anyway, what's he going to do? If he masturbates, that's sinful; there's no out for him, or for her.

I think sexual liberation means an awareness of a woman as a sexual being, as a part of her being a full person, a recognition of her sexual drives and needs. You know, there was a day when if a woman had strong sexual drives, it was thought she was a slut, all kinds of descriptions worse than that. She was supposed to be reserved. I think for a male, an awareness of a woman's sexual needs isn't either a paternalistic exercise or an exercise in getting his rocks off, but is an awareness of a relationship between two people. Inevitably, I think, this leads toward love or loving, even if you don't talk about it. For it seems to me that loving incarnates that respect for and awareness of another person. And, of course, this does bring homosexuality into the picture, since five to ten pecent of people in our society are counted as being homosexual. It means no longer having one's sex in a closet, dirty, faggoty, shadowy stuff; jack-off, suck, fuck, do it in the subway, do it in the toilet, feel awful, have no esteem. You know, smile and go to a dinner party and report for work in the morning, but go back to the Greyhound terminal, to the toilet; lie, lie, tell a lie for Christ; hate yourself, hate other people, use people as sex objects. It means bringing a light and health and wholeness into that situation. And in terms of the total sexual view, it's quite revolutionary because it turns all the tables around; it gets rid of a great many stereotypes. The macho male disappears; the woman as daddy's little girl or hot number disappears; the idea of the good and the bad woman disappears, the good woman as the wife, and the bad woman as when the guy has to go out and get his rocks off because the good woman isn't exciting enough—or he doesn't want her to be. Of course, I feel that victim in all this was the heterosexual macho male, who was about as macho as Shirley Temple, playing his little role, wearing his double-breasted suit, lugging his briefcase around, having to perform all day, every place, and my God, in bed, too. Never an end to performance, in a sense. But having said this, one has, you know, attacked cement cornerstones of our culture.

*Indeed, one of the cement cornerstones of our culture is the Church, and you have said that your sexual development has occurred as part of your religious experience. Isn't that an heretical position?*

Not in terms of God or religion, but in terms of organized religion and the institutional Church, yes.

*But doesn't that institutional Church condone only two types of sexual being in the world—heterosexual marriage or celibacy?*

Yeah.

*And you mentioned before that at least five to ten percent of the population is gay. What about the five to ten percent in the churches?*

It's not five to ten percent in the churches. In the Roman Catholic and Episcopal churches in the major cities, it's about thirty to sixty percent.

*Among the clergy?*

Yes. In the Episcopal Church, that includes a number of married clergy.

*Where does that leave these people?*

It makes a complete farce out of what the Church has been saying, because it hasn't pastorally been speaking to its own members. This includes, of course, the homosexual bishops and the church leaders who are still wearing iron masks, telling lies, suffering themselves, and contributing to the suffering of other people. Celibacy is something that I affirm and recognize, when valid. And it's very sexual; it's sexier than Elizabeth Taylor in *Cat on a Hot Tin Roof,* when valid. Because celibacy, when real, means taking one's sex and doing something with it, very specifically, looking at it close up and understanding it totally, genital and otherwise. And it's not a lie, it is a use that a certain number of people are able, with total honesty, to make of their sexuality. This is not in any sense restricted to nuns, priests, and others. There are certain people scattered through, honeycombed in society, who are legitimately celibate. I think it's a relatively small number, and I dread to think of the proportion of people who are professionally celibate. In other words, people in religious vocations who say they are, but who aren't, and who are subject to sexual fantasies and masturbate and who probably have furtive sex.

*Is furtive sex among the clergy very common?*

Very common, yes, and I think the only thing wrong about it is the lie that those clergy are forced to tell. Because I think to live a lie, to tell a lie at that level, especially when one is doing sexual counseling to other people, is very serious. But more than the counseling—then when do the lies stop? And how much self-respect is there? I know a lot of clergy: Baptist, Methodist, Roman Catholic, Episcopal, up and down the list, including most of the denominations, who don't have a great deal of self-respect, who have a kind of distorted view, like the priest who goes off and sleeps with an organist, or another priest, or whomever, but who is doing it in a furtive, lying way, who risks being caught or blackmailed, who is nervous, who really isn't open. I'd like that to end. I think that's very bad for everybody involved.

*Do you foresee an end to this?*

I don't know right now, because institutionalized religion isn't responding to ending it. Where I cannot take seriously the Church's admonitions on this level is the fact that I know that the Church was a whore wearing a clerical collar in civil rights and the peace movement, with very few exceptions. The Church that has been so immoral in relationship to women, blacks, war, can't suddenly put on a veil of morality and start instructing me. It has first to confess its sins, ask for absolution from God quite publicly, and look at the question of sexuality with more honesty. I'm shocked to remember that in 1900, a religious book was issued, *The Negro a Beast*, and it pointed out that black people didn't have souls and therefore couldn't be baptized. The Church has not been moral. I wish it to be moral, but I don't think that moral can mean 'tell a lie for Christ'. The Church is saying that to seminarians who are gay. 'It's all right for you to be gay; tell your bishop, tell a few superiors, and then lie for Christ; hide it, live your hidden, sequestered life, get your sex furtively, on the side'. And those seminarians who are not lying, but telling the truth, they're not being ordained.

*How do the leading Church authorities, both within the Episcopal Church and other churches, respond to you now that you have publicly declared yourself?*

In any number of ways. I'm in a curious place. I didn't become well-known because I announced that I'm gay. I have been a well-known person for some twenty years, so I'm familiar to most of the Church leadership. I've addressed national groups of most denominations, I guess. I addressed the U.S. Catholic bishops, assembled in Washington, D.C.

*Do you expect a return invitation?*

(Laughs) No, I don't. On the other hand, I don't know what to expect.

*How would you respond to those who view homosexuality as a perversion?*

I would respect them, because if this is what they've been taught, how can they know anything else? If they've been taught this is what the Bible says, that this is degeneracy, that this is the fall for Western civilization, the best way I can respond to them is by my own lifestyle, living as honestly as I can, and also trying to lead them to see the witness in other lives, and read some relevant literature. I don't deny respect to people who have different views. I'm a little astonished at some people who find that I have a different view and who therefore wish to deny me respect. I'm also curious about this admonition that every Christian is supposed to love the sinner while hating the sin; well, okay then, from the standpoint of some people, homosexuality is a sin, and as a homosexual, I am a sinner. I haven't observed much love from them.

*You taped a TV spot in which you voiced your opposition to the Briggs Amendment on the ballot in California. Do you see the Briggs Amendment as part of an ominous trend in the country, moving against the homosexual movement?*

What's ominous—again, this has nothing to do essentially with homosexuality—is that it's witch hunting, a new McCarthyism; it's cheap, third-rate, political demagogues who can't make their points against fairly good politicians, the standard things that would win, unless they have the gimmickry to do something kind of dirty. A Jew is an important political scapegoat in this society, explicitly; I suppose the Jew is a damn good implicit scapegoat everywhere else. I was just rereading material on the Dreyfus Affair in France. But probably, right now, the best scapegoat is the homosexual and homosexuality itself. It's ripe because there really has not been a great deal of information. There is misunderstanding, I feel, between the messages of the women's movement, the gay movement, and others in intransigent positions. There is the fear of touching a sexual nerve in this society, and, on top of it, there is the problem of new works dealing with homosexuality completely being denied access in the media, in many cases. All this, added up, is a damned good field for demagogues. I have enough respect for the American political system and the American people to foresee a turnabout on this. It came in California with the defeat of the Briggs Amendment. Incidentally, I'd like to say that I think Wichita, St. Paul, Eugene, Miami, all the places where gays have lost, I see as quite a victory. And so I see future losses as victories, too, because instead of being the unmentionable leper, thanks to two people like Anita Bryant and Briggs, it's hot stuff on the CBS Evening News and the front page of your friendly newspaper. So, in other words, the issue is now wide open. It's been marvelous that these people have ironically served this purpose. I would say it's the will of God. (laughs)

*In reading* Take Off the Masks, *I was struck by a statement you made about trying to escape the truth. 'Vainly,' you wrote, 'having to escape, even from death, one rudely discovers that one has an appointment in Samarra after all.' Which reminded me of a saying of Horace's: 'I shall not altogether die, my sublimations shall exalt me to the stars.' Is there not a mutually reinforcing relationship between the fear of death and the fear of sex?*

I guess undoubtedly there is, yes. Sex in all of its mystery can go either—well, can go a lot of ways—but basically, I guess, it can be accommodating and accommodative. Never leading to full openness, never giving oneself, one can have a kind of conventional sex. I feel that true sexuality involves a lot of risk, an opening up of oneself, giving, sharing, lack of pretense. So it's a given that has a bottom-line quality and, God knows, death does, too. Now how one would approach death in that conventional way, I have no idea. On the other

hand, if one has approached sex that way, perhaps one under-
stands how to approach death that way, too. I can't approach
anything that way because that would mean that dying was
something casual—which in a social sense, it is, of course—
but it would mean that in terms of one's own dying, that one
could fit it in between, you know, (laughs) four and six
o'clock, and not inconvenience the family if they're leaving
for Egypt. And presumably, one would be drugged and there
wouldn't be any sweaty moment in dying, one wouldn't shit
in bed or, God forbid, fart.

*Has your 'coming out' adversely affected your professional opportu-
nities within the Church, the publishing world, etc.?*

I find that a hard question to answer. From the standpoint of
opportunities in the field of religion, they'd already been
limited quite a lot by my activities in civil rights and against
the war, meaning I was known as a barn burner or not a very
safe establishment type. I could never be trusted with the
party line, because it never came first, and so naturally this
cut opportunities in that respect. With the broader public
role, it's almost too early to say. I'm receiving a number of
invitations that are fascinating, which I'm enjoying, and I
love them—these in the broader, not the narrower, religious
sphere. I'm talking about public speaking, visits to colleges
and universities, this kind of thing. And this is done in full
awareness of myself as Malcolm Boyd which includes a number of things, including being gay. In publishing, it's
knocked me out for the moment. I don't exactly know where
to go next, and I've never been in this position before; I don't
particularly like it. I'm getting so much advice from everybody. In other words, everybody knows that I'm gay, and
that's okay, but why don't you knock off the gay subject next
time. Or why don't you precisely and deliberately do a gay

subject, ergo this one. But what it's forcing me to do is try to knock off the public role completely and figure out what I, as a person, really do want to write next. But that gets complicated because I *am* a responsible person, and I'm always interested in and concerned about what would be of use to other people, as well as just myself. So I find myself going in circles a little bit here.

I recently chatted with Alex Haley; we had a good talk. I like him very much. And he said that it's much harder for him now to write in terms of his particular public role; he's in demand, there are image expectations, all that kind of thing. I think mostly it's a matter of time, and it's hard for him to get away and, I guess, just write now, what with the demands pouring in. I have all kinds of demands pouring in and people wanting me for here, there, and everywhere— people wanting to see me, to talk to me. And added to that is the question of my wishing to be responsible about my work. In other words, I'm not just an isolated individual who can be selfish. This is causing me a lot of trouble in terms of creativity. I may decide to start two or three writing projects at once that are quite different from each other, and work on them as I wish. And they'll be quite different things. All three, presumably, will be completed. And they could go to different publishers, and conceivably different readerships would be interested in them.

Recently, I reread James Baldwin's *Nobody Knows My Name*. That, and *Notes of a Native Son* are his two best books, in my opinion, although some would feel that *Go Tell It on the Mountain* and, perhaps, *Giovanni's Room* are. But I felt a purity of prose in him at that time; he excited me. Now, Baldwin became a public person, a political person. Ironically, he never wrote so well again. Or was it the commercial packaging of Baldwin that got in the way? Or was it the unresolved gayness? I don't mean that he's been closeted or quiet about it, but I mean blacks made it rather obvious that he shouldn't be black as well as gay, or I should say gay as well as black, since black he is, primarily. What happened to Baldwin as a writer is something I've thought about a lot lately, in terms of where I go myself.

*You seem to be caught between two conflicting worlds . . .*

At least . . .

*Yes, at least. But on one hand, the gay community would like you to throw off the religious role and attachments that you have, while on the other hand, the religious community would like you to throw off your gayness.*

I wish it were even that simple. For example, there is no gay community; the gay world, the gay universe, is very diverse, with many conflicting egos, with many conflicting points of view. There is one very strong anti-religious motif running through the gay movement, and I understand it, I share it. I mean rage is understandable when one considers what has happened in the name of religion, in terms of murders and tortures and deaths. And yet, *Blueboy Magazine,* a leading gay magazine, printed three poems of mine recently, including one about a closeted homosexual bishop. I go from here to St. Louis in about a week to speak at a religiously-sponsored, city-wide gay meeting. And then I'll address several thousand people in Los Angeles, at what is essentially a religiously oriented gay rally. So you have lots of complexity here underneath labels. In the religious world, organized religion would certainly like my gayness to go away, and yet if I have anything to say now to many religious people, it is something about my being gay and being able to be honest about that to literally millions of gay religious people. So I find that this is profoundly complex because there are so many cracks in this particular goal.

*Do you think that you will be forced to leave the institutional church?*

I don't know. Attempts *have* been made already to force me to leave, and these have been rejected by equally strong or stronger groups within the Church. So if organized religion tried to remove me, I would at a point have to say I don't recognize the validity of organized religion to do so. I stand, in my own view, beneath the validity of God, which cannot be equated with that of organized religion. I can't respect the morality of organized religion; I respect the morality of God. So I don't know what that would even mean, if that particular controversy is yet to be lived through. Having lived under the tyranny and slavery of so many things throughout my life, I'm at a point now where I'm a kind of thorny, difficult person in a lot of ways. I don't take public-relations marching orders from a publisher, a church, anyone in the gay world; I wish to maintain as much integrity and dignity as I can for the remainder of my life. And that means I don't take marching orders from anybody else.

*Do you think that there's a liberal attitude prevailing today, say in New York and San Francisco, that says in effect: 'We've done our bit, aired the whole gay issue, and now let's give it a rest?'*

Unquestionably, this is true, I think. Even when I came out two years ago, I was astonished that a very 'liberal" minister in New York preached a sermon in which he mentioned that I'd come out, and then he asked for a moratorium for a while on anyone else coming out. I think, presumably, this would be met by polite laughter and assent. The other tragedy for gays is that hardly anybody has come out, you could almost say nobody has come out. I mean, look at prominent fields. I was thinking for a while of writing a novel in which the premise would be that about twelve very well-known people, a leading star, a leading White House aide, a leading magazine editor—that gets a little close for comfort (laughs)—a leading religious figure, indeed a bishop, a very prominent writer, a Pentagon general, all these people would come out together. They're all there. They haven't come out, and they're not going to come out, and the liberal attitude in New York and San Francisco is a little like the *Time* Magazine cover psychology. You know, blacks get a cover; Jews get a cover; Arab oil men get a cover; Hungarian refugees get a cover; Charlie Chaplin gets a cover; and then kind of go away and shut up because we did it. Also, to continue appearing liberal, having done the cover in effect, liberals need to get on to ever-new causes in order to continue to appear liberal. And I think liberals in New York and San Francisco, although they say they despise Des Moines and Tulsa, want to be considered liberal there, want to be admired, and want to represent the avant-garde. And what quickly becomes old hat in New York and San Francisco is seen in those places as being old hat elsewhere. For blacks, this presented a problem. I remember reading once in a story about the publishing of books by blacks and about blacks, by leading New York publishers, a very prominent editor said, and was quoted by Time: 'Black is no longer chic.' He meant, in effect, the same thing about black as you intimated in your question about gay, and that his house wouldn't be publishing very many more books either by or about blacks.

For gays, this has been near disastrous, the fact that there are people who consider themselves liberal in New York and

San Francisco, who feel that their liberalism involves having gays to cocktail parties and to dinners and all over the place. This is now a fait accompli, this is really over; let's get on to something else. But it's not over at all, it never really began. And I think this is why a number of people, including me, have lacked certain reviews that they needed. I think it's why the condition of gays is really in quite a lot of jeopardy. I'm not paranoid, and I don't intend to be. I'm aware that if a power shift did happen in this country, that I'm in all the FBI files in terms of civil rights and anti-war demonstrations and arrests, and I kind of think the files are not dead. And also that being gay just might become a regressive thing and take on some sinister meanings at any political moment, depending upon the scapegoat issue. There is this little corner of my mind that could have me seated in a prison cell because I have risked a great deal and am a very vulnerable person. I know many friends who feel that the society is going to go that way, or even worse, and I'm aware 1984 approaches, and I recently reread the book. I see where we are economically and a number of other ways. I know the sell-out by Carter. And despite all this, I remain pretty much on the upbeat about it. One reason is I'm aware of the danger of self-fulfilling prophecy. I like my energies to be positive rather than negative. In a sense, the picture I hold in my own mind of the future of society might have something to do with that very future.

*That brings up the question of the present and the immediate past, and I'm wondering if you have suffered any harassment from whatever quarter since you have 'come out'.*

To answer the question, I'm going to have to give an analogy. Let's say that someone has been living in the country and moves into the inner city of New York. The noise level and the sound level increase rapidly, and you ask the person something about quietness. In a way, the person no longer remembers because the quality of life, in terms of the noise or sound level, has increased so rapidly and to such an extent that that person is caught in a new experience. So many things have happened to one since coming out, that it's almost difficult for me to remember back to when they weren't happening. And I'm wondering if I'm responding to them correctly. For example, I'm someone whose books were generally reviewed by an awful lot of people. Here I have probably the major book of my life, and a book, I think, of great social significance, not being reviewed very much. And I'm finding that this is the norm. And there's abusive mail. Obviously, at one point in my life, there was no abusive mail; then in civil rights, there was the letter saying you're a nigger, and this kind of thing—a little scary, also a little removed, a little remote. I was very afraid of some mail at a point in the anti-war movement when it got to be vicious. And I became somewhat paranoid. As a matter of fact, the FBI did arrive once at a house that I was visiting. I had just flown in from Yale, where I was a fellow, and this guy from the FBI arrived and asked if I was shielding Daniel Berrigan in the house; that was the period when Dan was a refugee. Things like that were a little scary. But then I learned to live with that, and in the hundreds of letters—I guess thousands of letters in all now—there have been some awfully abusive ones, but the vast majority are not, they're quite the opposite. But it means I'm living on a different level. For years, there's been a certain recognition from television and the news, and I'm used to that. I'm not Robert Redford or Raquel Welch, so it's not at that level at all. It was, briefly, after *Are You Running with Me, Jesus?,* but that's calmed down now. But recently, I walked into an airport—I think it was Atlanta, but that doesn't really matter—and I got ten very hot, deliberate, long looks, and I was alone, waiting to board

Malcolm Boyd in a dance group, Detroit, 1962.

a plane, and the people didn't look away; there was a lot of anger, resentment in some of them. One was friendly, he was a Roman Catholic seminarian. On the plane, he came over and wished to talk to me. This takes a certain amount of energy. Friends have suggested that I shouldn't go into certain, say, rural southern areas by myself. I don't know. I mean, on a level you want to laugh, so you don't sound either like Kafka or Jules Feiffer or a cheap dime novel. But then understanding the element of violence in our society and the extraordinary power of the media, it's hard to know what precisely to make of some things.

There was something that happened in San Francisco; it's bizarre. My lover and I had been living in an apartment, but we had moved two days before. In the apartment house, an old ramshackle house in a lower-class black ghetto and a lower-to-middle-class gay ghetto, there was a young woman and her baby and some other people who aren't relevant to the story. Well, one night at one o'clock in the morning, the young mother and baby were awakened by some banging on the door and shouts, and she went to the window, and two men—uniformed policemen, were there, and there was a police car, and they called up, 'Is Malcolm Boyd here?' And she said no. They said the telephone listed in my name was in some way interfering with a police transmitter. Well, the phone wasn't listed in my name to begin with. Secondly, if the police had checked, they would have found that the number had been changed to a new number where we were living. And they said that there was an emergency and they had to find me. Well, I never heard from them again. In other words, in the morning, the emergency had evaporated. They didn't look me up. What's scary about a situation like that is this was a run-down dwelling place in a run-down neighborhood. And for years, I've been aware that in a number of cities, the police have arrived at such places—usually blacks are there or chicanos are there, gays are there—and the police enter, people are sleeping, and they're enraged, they're scared, they overreact, and usually there can be something of a violent nature. The police generally make an arrest on the basis of having been attacked by someone who thought he/she was protecting himself/herself. It's something that has all the makings of unpleasantness and danger, and so I followed that up with the Chief of Police and the Mayor and everybody else. The police department couldn't find any record of the squad car that had been there. Now I'm a well-known gay person, my book was out, I had been on national television; you don't know what to make of these things. But they're out of the ordinary, and in my life, the out-of-the-ordinary may loom larger than the ordinary, and I am perhaps becoming accustomed to it, and that's dangerous. I don't like it, but I have no choice, it's something happening to me.

*As you face the future, and as many young gay people face theirs, what are your hopes and expectations for well-known gay people to serve as role models for younger gays?*

The term 'role model' is itself a controversial and a tough one. Very few people, I think, want to be role models for anyone, and yet in a number of areas, there are certain well-known chicanos, blacks, women—up and down the ladder—people in opera, athletics, and so one, who are role models simply because of who and where they are. And I know one reason I felt it was essential to come out is that if in some small way I could help alleviate the intense suffering of millions of people, I wished to do so. If I could preclude one more suicide by a homosexual, well, if I could just do *anything,* because I'm aware of the degree of suffering, which is enormous. And there are two kinds of people who don't talk about the suffering much these days: one, a professional gay apologist who wants to make it all sound like Disneyland; and the others are Anita Bryants, et. al. who try to look at a big social sin but don't want to impart any information about individuals who are suffering because of what they're doing. I simply don't know what to say about people coming out; they haven't been. And some of the best-known people I know who are homosexual—I don't use the word 'gay' deliberately because these are closeted people—what I gather from them is that they wish, in a way, that they could come out but have no intention of doing so; they don't want to lose their income; they don't want to lose their corporate status, wherever it is; they don't want to confront a parent, wife, husband, father, mother, son, daughter, nephew, anybody; they don't want to rock the boat; they don't want to be caught in controversy, and they can get a few goodies on the side. It's not simple for them. Many have a drinking problem, many are just really unhappy, but they're content to ride it out. And also, the direct result of some of the anti-gay political activity across the country has been a victory for anti-gays; in other words, it has driven a number of homosexuals deeper, I think, into the honeycombs. And yet I get mail from young homosexuals, women and men, and these are really poignant letters, and they don't know what to do, some are coming out in a very natural way, and it seems very okay mentally and physically. I'm delighted.

*With all the difficulties you've encountered and are encountering within the Church, I wonder why you don't leave.*

It would be much simpler for a great many people if I did. I was half amused and half hurt by a review of *Masks* in the *Soho Weekly News*. The writer, apparently a very strong anti-religious gay, felt that I kept on an ultimate mask by not leaving the Church, and I was guilty of a very deep hypocrisy in talking about taking off masks when I didn't take that one off. I could really have the adulation and acceptance of anti-religious gays and probably of a number of Church leaders (laughs) if I'd remove myself from the Church and take a jet somewhere. But I've never taken a simplistic approach in my life. I'm also not in a popularity contest, never have been and never will be, and I'm a multi-faceted person. A part of me and a part of who I am is the struggle that I have with religion—God knows I'm not the first—look at history. But it's a struggle à la Virginia Woolf, part of my life, that particular marriage, that will go on; it's creative, it has a lot of meaning. It would be a very sorrowful thing, I think, for someone like myself to remove himself in a kind of simplistic gesture from the Church and thereby deny not only a struggle but a possible resolution that might make sense for a great number of people. Also, why should I leave the Church to the people running it? I get a little tired of critics of the Church, who include those of us who have the guts to stay in and confront the Church from within. The people who confront it from outside are no danger to the Church at all; the Church can laugh them off. It is those of us who are within who know the fabric and who have power of a kind, who force issues and, I think, meaningful and creative conflict. Also, I don't want to deny or minimize the diversity of myself, I don't want to be a simple homogenized person; I'm very complicated. I'd like it to have been more so. That's paying a homage to life. I refuse to be a vegetable, either by lying about my sexual orientation or by accommodating critics who would like me, if I could, to become a vegetable or conform to their image requirements. I won't amend myself.

*Earlier, we agreed that the issue that we're discussing is not simply homosexuality, but sexuality. What would you see as a sexually responsible and joyful way for a person to relate to others?*

In the first place, not to be fearful of one's own or anyone else's sexuality, not to put a fence around the area that has 'SEX' written on it, and also maybe a sign, 'Don't touch. Don't get within five feet!' This means accepting that sex is a part of human life—in my view, God-created and God-given human life. Sex is good, sex is healthful. Of course, it can be misused, as can religion, alcohol, or politics. But we're talking here about positive and healthful use. This means also not asking anyone else to conform to one's own views or rules of sexuality, but accepting that—not just accepting—wanting other people to run the full gamut of sexuality, in terms of their own feelings and nature and experience and needs. We need to understand sexuality as something natural, rather than forced. We are so hung up about it as a society, it seems to me. We deny its naturalness, we try to program it all the time. And sexuality takes many forms other than intercourse. There is sexuality in the way two people walk up the street or look at a tree or have lunch, listen to music. I think we should open ourselves to that sexuality. And I think if each of us felt secure and confident and happy and healthful in our sexuality, this is the best beginning I can think of, because then we can communicate this to somebody else and also receive communication from someone else. This means a much more relaxed attitude toward oneself and others. And I think orgasm, or scoring, or coming, or whatever it's called, is best when it fits into a natural context. One doesn't have to 'perform' or be 'on stage' in sex. I'm very much in favor of relating loving and sex, which means I'm anti-rape. And I think sex can meet a lot of needs at levels of two people coming together and being together, rather than being alone. Tennessee Williams has that great line in *Camino Real:* 'In a place like this where so many are lonely, it would be inexcusably selfish to be lonely alone.' There's a lot to that.

There's a story I read that had a lot of meaning—it was in jail, in prison someplace—a woman had been tortured, her humanness denied, including her femaleness, and a male guard managed to get into her cell and make love to her, and this gave her the strength to survive the rest of the torture. They met years later, casually. She was married and a political figure, but to me that story says something. And I think to attempt to put sex under a label—in other words, nuclear family or missionary position (laughs) or coupling or marriage, or whatever—is simplistic; it can be very wrong. Also, a lot of people under the labels are very unhappy and very unfulfilled and not recognizing their potential or themselves as sexual persons. And to recognize oneself as such doesn't mean bang! bang!, but it means making love. And one isn't going to have intercourse with everybody, but one can make fun or love with a lot of people if one is a willing person. And that doesn't mean . . . I'm not talking about foreplay on a bus. I'm talking about an attitude and a way of reacting to people, of liking them, of being interested in them, of looking at their full selves and relating. I'd like to see a cutting down of fearfulness and fences and rules and puritan judgmental narrowness. I think the potential for a full awareness and realization of sexuality is as important as anything else, and I think it is very, very limited in this society.

Published in paper wrappers and a hardcover trade edition. There is a specially bound hardcover edition of 26 lettered and signed copies.